STRATEGIES FOR SUNDAY SCHOOL GROWTH

George A. Edgerly
Harold E. Crosby

Gospel Publishing House
Springfield, Missouri

02-0591

STRATEGIES FOR SUNDAY SCHOOL GROWTH

This is a Workers Training Division textbook. Credit for its study will be issued under Classification 1, Sunday School Department, Assemblies of God.

Library of Congress Catalog Card Number 83-080404
International Standard Book Number 0-88243-591-4
Printed in the United States of America

Foreword

"The decade of church growth." "The Church will explode in the 80s." "This is the Church's finest hour." These and other resounding superlatives are being expressed all around us. Recent exposure of the evangelical and charismatic segments of Christianity to the public has occurred. "The Year of the Evangelical" has been proclaimed. *Time, Newsweek,* and *U.S. News & World Report* have given attention to the charismatic renewal and phenomenal church growth of the 70s. Television networks have shown documentaries on the subject. Books have been written. There have been conferences by the score along with a proliferation of magazines and tapes dedicated to the subject of church growth.

Most of the recent attention deals with the how-to areas of growth. Much of the expertise is creative and has stimulated pastors, ministers of Christian Education, and Sunday school workers to bring fulfillment to Jesus' mandate to the church to reach out and grow.

This book, *Strategies for Sunday School Growth* by George Edgerly and Harold Crosby, takes us a step further. It analyzes the *why* and not only gives a workable formula for growth but also an in-depth study setting forth positive reasons for people being added to church rolls.

This book deals with the role of the Sunday school in church growth. I believe the authors have produced a study that is needed by both our own Assemblies of God fellowship and the body of Christ in general.

Foreword

In recent years, growth seems to have been stimulated by worship and evangelism in the corporate body. Some pastors believe worship is the key to growth and some have discarded adult Sunday school entirely. My instinct tells me the past is prologue. Sunday school has served the Church well for 200 years. With the beauty of worship bringing people to the corporate body, the Sunday school will help keep them there.

We must reach and teach, calling people to decisions and then making them disciples. Given to the Church is the responsibility to both educate and evangelize. In my judgment, our two authors have done a service to the Kingdom by providing inspiration, instruction, and explanation for growth.

ERNEST J. MOEN
PASTOR
FIRST ASSEMBLY OF GOD
ROCKFORD, ILLINOIS

Contents

1

Why Assemblies of God
Sunday Schools Are Growing

It has been an exciting decade for the Assemblies of God. From humble beginnings in Hot Springs, Arkansas in 1914, our fellowship now numbers more than 10,000 churches in the U.S. As we approach our seventieth birthday there are many evidences of God's continuing blessings. Our world-wide constituency is now more than 12 million.

The growth of the Assemblies of God in particular, and the Pentecostal movement in general, is akin to that of the first century church. And perhaps the emphasis upon New Testament Christianity—trying to copy the message, methods, and motivation of the Early Church—is producing the same results.

During the 70s our membership increased by 70 percent. In the same period many of the older denominations experienced alarming losses. Three of the ten largest churches (based on total membership) in the world are Assemblies of God. And the rise of the "super-sized" congregation in the U.S. is equally dramatic. In 1971, only two Assemblies of God Sunday schools averaged more than 1,000 in attendance. In 1981, 48 were over that mark—three with a weekly attendance of 4,000 plus. It took 37 years for our first Sunday school to break the thousand barrier. During the 70s we saw the 2,000, 3,000, 4,000 and then 5,000 marks fall quickly.

However, it is not just big churches that are growing. A majority of our present 10 largest schools were not even in the 100 largest listings a few years ago. Calvary Temple, Springfield, Illinois, did not exist until the late 60s. Under the leadership of its founding pastors, Reverend and Mrs. M. C. Johnson, it had grown to an average of 5,000 plus by 1980. Westside Assembly of God in Davenport, Iowa, under the leadership of Reverend Tommy Barnett, grew from an average of 78 in 1971 to a peak of nearly 5,000 within 10 years. Equally dramatic gains have been registered by First Assembly of God, Rockford, Illinois; First Assembly of God, Grand Rapids, Michigan; First Assembly of God, New Orleans, Louisiana; First Assembly of God, Lakeland, Florida; Calvary Assembly, Winter Park, Florida; First Assembly of God, Phoenix, Arizona; Central Assembly of God, Joplin, Missouri; Crossroads Cathedral, Oklahoma City, Oklahoma; Huffman Assembly of God, Birmingham, Alabama; Calvary Community Church, San Jose, California; Lakeview Temple, Indianapolis, Indiana, and many more. All of these have broken both the 1,000 and the 2,000 plateaus since 1971.

The explosive growth of these churches has given them high visibility, not only in our fellowship, but in the greater church world. Their accomplishments have benefited all of our churches. They have broken psychological barriers and helped others see that growth is not only possible, but also attainable. They have pioneered concepts of outreach and organization that have been adapted and effectively used by others. Reports of their explosive growth have provided a positive image for our entire fellowship.

Perhaps nothing has dramatized the continued growth of the Assemblies of God nationwide more than the dominance of the International Christian Education Association's annual growth awards. At their annual convention in Detroit, Michigan, the ICEA attempts to discover the fastest growing Sunday school in each of the 50 states. In 1982, 24 of the awards went to Assemblies of God Sunday schools.

In size and influence, the Assemblies of God has taken a recognized place among the churches of America. Once rejected as being "across the tracks" and ridiculed for supposed doctrinal aberrations, the Assemblies of God today have a respected position among evangelicals.

The growth of God's kingdom through the Assemblies of God is much greater than can be measured by a comparison of our attendance figures. The witness of Pentecostal congregations has been used by God to spark revival in many different denominations. The recently completed *World Christian Encyclopedia* by David Barnett reveals that the largest segment of Protestantism is now Pentecostals. Worldwide, Pentecostal believers are at least 62 million strong.

Two recent articles in major publications have brought national attention to the growth of the Assemblies of God. In the July/August, 1982 *Saturday Evening Post,* Edward Plowman, wrote an article titled "Assemblies of God, On the Way Up." In it he wrote, "Today (the Assemblies of God) is on the leading edge of the evangelical wing of Christianity, and it is one of the fastest growing church bodies on earth."

In the January 7, 1983, issue of *Christianity Today,* Dean Merril commented, "Church watchers may have suspected as much, but two new statistical studies make it clear: the fastest growing denomination in America is the Assemblies of God."

The recently published decadal study of church membership, compiled by the Glenmary Foundation, reveals that one of the strengths of the Assemblies of God is our distribution. While our concentration of churches is still in the southcentral states (28 percent of our churches are located in the four adjacent states of Texas, Oklahoma, Arkansas, and Missouri) there is an Assemblies of God congregation in 79 percent of the counties in the U.S. In many major cities the largest evangelical church is an Assembly of God. In a 1979 research project conducted by Dr. Terry Lewis and George Edgerly, it was discovered that there were two geographical concentrations among the 115 fastest growing Assemblies— Southern Florida and the industrial northeast of New England and New York. Aggressive church planting is producing dramatic results east of the Mississippi.

We dare not become chauvinistic, or unduly proud of what we are through no merit of our own. God does not require that everyone be Assemblies of God in order to please Him. Likewise, we must not be tempted to believe that we have "arrived." We must realize how far we have to go instead of resting on past laurels. It is obvious that the greatest opportunities we have ever known lie just ahead. God is building His Church. The real question is, "Will we, individually, be the kind of church that He can bless?"

Dean Merril comments in his article in *Christianity Today*, "Outside observers notice that the Assemblies have not soured on Sunday school." While many denominations de-emphasized Christian education, we have continued to contend for balance between evangelism and education. While it is true that the Sunday school is not the dominant tool of evangelism and outreach that it was in the 50s, it is still a strong contributor both in reaching and maturing new people.

Ernest Moen, pastor of First Assembly of God, Rockford, Illinois, declares that Christian education is the hub on which the wheel of the church turns. "Church and Sunday school go together like love and marriage," Moen declared while speaking at the Michigan District Sunday School Convention in the fall of 1982.

I recently asked Norman Wenig, pastor of First Assembly, Burlington, Iowa, how important Sunday school has been to the growth of the church he pastors. "Absolutely indispensable," he replied without hesitation.

While there are many Assemblies, both large and small, with more dramatic stories than First Assembly, Burlington, Iowa, it is in many ways typical of what is happening in so many of our churches. Wenig accepted the pastorate in 1970 after serving as Iowa district youth and Sunday school director for 5 years.

In thirteen years the church in Burlington has grown from an average attendance of only eighty to more than five hundred each week. There has been a consistent increase each year with the exception of the year they suffered a facilities crunch.

Rachel Perry, who, with her husband John, directs First Assembly Christian Academy, Burlington, Iowa, observes that the secret has been workers. Wenig borrowed an idea from James Mayo, Sr., then pastor of the Assembly of God Tabernacle in Atlanta, Georgia. He put two teachers in every class. When he introduced the idea to his people, they laughed. It had been difficult to keep one teacher in each class, let alone two. But the concept of team teaching, coupling an apprentice with an experienced teacher, proved to be a winner. It was easier to recruit a "helper" than someone to take full responsibility. Discipline was improved. There was more effective teaching time since the "helper" could handle the time consuming duties of taking roll, counting the offering, etc.

Not only that, when the class grew—Wenig kept a firm commitment to small classes in the elementary and preschool departments despite a growing bus ministry—and when it needed to be divided, there was a teacher for the new class who had already built relationships with the children. A new apprentice was appointed for each class and the process of on-the-job training along with workers conferences and training programs rolled on.

Space quickly became a problem. The 2-year-old church building was adequate only for a Sunday school of 125 average. But pastor and people decided they could provide additional space. Creative scheduling was introduced. The beginners and primaries used the auditorium for their children's church during the Sunday school hour. The auditorium class, made up of senior adults, remodeled the parsonage garage for their class. While the little tables and chairs remained in place in the younger children's classrooms, the youth classes used them for their class. As the youth left they carried out their folding chairs and stacked them, leaving the classrooms ready for the smaller children.

The cafeteria of the local junior high school was rented for the pastor's young adult class. The church board agreed to pay Pastor Wenig a housing allowance so the parsonage could be used for class space. "I had to agree that the allowance wouldn't be paid any month we didn't make the budget," Wenig recalls. "I haven't missed one yet. Every move forward requires a step of faith on someone's part!" The old parsonage at the former church downtown became the junior department Sunday school and junior church. The buses unloaded the other children at the church, picked up the junior age children who came with their parents, and transported them all to the old parsonage for the full Sunday morning program. So that the bus children who did not attend evening services would know who the pastor was, Wenig always led their junior church one Sunday each month while his co-teacher led the young adult class.

Of course there are new buildings today. A lovely sanctuary was followed by a gym and facilities which are used for both their Christian school and the Sunday morning services. Paid staff has been added. But the thrust of First Assembly is still to do the basics of outreach, evangelism, follow-up, teaching, and training; and growth continues.

Shirley, New York, is halfway out on Long Island, about 1½ hours on the commuter train from Manhattan. Pastor James Raynor grew up in neighboring Center Moriches but was not part of the Assemblies of God until his conversion in the Navy. He became involved in missionary outreaches to children on Okinawa. Several of the outreach ministries to children that he and his fellow workers started have grown into Assemblies of God congregations.

Upon his return in 1961 he became involved as a layman in the Assembly in Center Moriches. In 1969 he accepted the leadership of the struggling church in neighboring Shirley. It then ran about 30 in Sunday school and worship. Today the Sunday school averages 337 and there are more than 600 in worship services.

Pastor Raynor says that Sunday school is the major

factor in the growth of his congregation. When asked how this could be true, considering that worship attendance is nearly double that of Sunday school, he replied, "It is the follow-up to family members of the people who we reach through Sunday school. Not only that, our Sunday school figures do not represent the total Christian education ministries we provide. Our Wednesday night adult electives have an average of 175 persons involved in Bible study and specific training for ministry. *Fundamentals for Sunday School Workers,* a four unit study for training potential Sunday school workers, is offered continually. So is training in evangelism and soul winning.

"Thursday nights we have an ongoing new converts class. When a new Christian has completed the six weeks study, he is enrolled in the Sunday morning 'New Life' class. Without a doubt Sunday school has contributed to every phase of our growth."

Pastor Raynor volunteered three major reasons for the growth of the church in Shirley.

1. *Vision for children.* "We believe we need to see them saved before we have to remake them." But reaching children is not an end in itself, it is the open door to reaching entire families. They realize the greatest ministry a church can have to a child is to reach his parents and allow him to grow up in a Christian home.

2. *Dedication of workers.* "It is a spiritual motivation," observed Pastor Raynor. "Only with this kind of commitment to Christ could our workers have put up with the conditions they have in order to minister to more people. For 3 years we had classes on the Sunday school buses—even in the winter. We used nearby restaurants and even had a class in a church closet. Even with the new facilities, dual scheduling means that some workers never get to attend morning worship because they teach two different classes each morning."

3. *Prayer.* "Our Saturday night prayer meeting is the dynamic force that makes it all work."

Other pastors might not credit Sunday school as strongly a factor of growth as does James Raynor. They would cite the emphasis upon worship as being the major reason for their rapid gains. But this does not mean that they have forsaken Sunday school. Often they have broadened their Christian education ministries to other times, places, and structures.

Representative of these churches would be Calvary Temple in Naperville, Illinois. It has been pastored by Robert Schmidgall for its entire 15 year history. Current worship attendance, in two separate morning services, is over 1800 while Sunday school averages 766.

"But we have not forsaken Sunday school," says Pastor Schmidgall. "We attract people through worship, but worship alone cannot produce stability. Stability and spiritual growth are produced through teaching ministries. Because of the characteristics of our community, we have difficulty in getting people, especially adults, to come to Sunday school. We realize that we must supplement Sunday school with many other Christian education ministries."

Scriptural Pattern for Church Growth

The great commission as given in Matthew 28:19,20 bears out the relationship between evangelism, worship, and Christian education. Jesus said,

> Go ye therefore, and teach all nations, baptizing them in the name of the Father, and of the Son, and of the Holy Ghost: teaching them to observe all things whatsoever I have commanded you: and, lo, I am with you alway, even unto the end of the world.

It must be obvious that Jesus was asking us for more than decisions. We must produce disciples. There is teaching that is necessary before conversion is possible. Paul wrote in Romans 10:14 "How then shall they call on him in whom they have not believed? and how shall they believe in him of whom they have not heard? and how shall they hear without a preacher?" But teaching people to repent, believe, and be baptized is incomplete unless we also commit ourselves to teach them to observe (that is, teaching them *how* to observe rather than *what* to observe) the teachings of Jesus.

"I will build my church!" That challenge of Jesus is not open for negotiation. He is building His Church. The question is, "Will we be a part of His Church?"

Ephesians 4:1-16 is a clear revelation of how Jesus is building that Church. In this passage Paul shows us the attitudes, authority, and administration necessary for any local congregation who is part of that Church, to grow.

Attitudes for Church Growth

The three major attitudes for church growth are commitment to service, to unity, and to truly love.

Paul had a right to call the Ephesians to a renewed commitment to service. He was a "prisoner of the Lord." Arrested on the Damascus road, he was the epitomy of "walk[ing] worthy of the vocation wherewith ye are called." One of the major crisis of church growth, and of Christian life itself, is whether we will be full-time servants of Jesus Christ. Our calling is not an avocation nor a vacation. It is our vocation—a commitment to a total Christian life-style—that should occupy all our time and effort.

To "walk worthy" means we must be both humble and patient. Pride and impatience are the two main destroyers of church unity. And unity is essential to growth. Jesus linked unity, the ability to "agree together," with the church's power. No church is too small to conduct business in Jesus' name if they are truly "together in my name," Jesus said. This is not a magical formula for answered prayer. It is the commitment of each believer to the overall purposes of the church. United believers set the gates of hell rattling.

However, a divided church is easily conquered. Satan gloats over church problems. He knows that disunity renders us spiritually powerless.

Authority for Church Growth

In Ephesians 4:7-11 Paul declares that we can be victorious because Christ won the victory for us. We can be used of God in building His Church, and challenging the powers of hell, because Christ has shared the spoils of His triumph over Satan.

Psalms 68:18 declares that when the Messiah would ascend for His coronation, He would receive gifts *for* men. It would seem contradictory that the King, upon His coronation, would give gifts instead of receiving them. But Jesus desires to equip His Church with the authority that He wrested from Satan through Calvary and the Resurrection.

Isaiah 53:12 says, "Therefore will I divide him a portion with the great, and he shall divide the spoil with the strong . . ." Colossians 2:15 declares that he "spoiled principalities and powers" (demonic forces). Luke 11:22 contains Jesus promise that He would conquer Satan, take away his armor, and divide the spoils with His friends.

Because Jesus won the battle over Satan's powers and plots, He can empower us to do it again. Jesus told His disciples, *"As my Father hath sent me,* even *so send I you"* (emphasis added). Then He breathed on them and told them to "Receive ye the Holy Ghost," (John 20:21, 22). Just as Jesus overcame Satan through the anointing of the Spirit, so He now equips the Church with the same spiritual gifts.

Administration for Church Growth

The gifts of the Spirit mentioned in Ephesians 4:11 (compare also Romans 12:6-8 and 1 Corinthians 12:8-10, 28-30) are used through divinely called and gifted men. The King James Version seems to indicate that the role of these gifted men is threefold—to perfect the saints, to do the work of ministry, and to build up the body of Christ (4:12). The New International Version translates it more accurately: ". . . to prepare God's people for works of service, so that the body of Christ may be built up."

The administrative gift (1 Corinthians 12:28 calls it "governments," Romans 12:8 describes it as ruling) should be possessed by the church leader so that he can help others discover their abilities, roles, and gifts.

God does not intend for the pastor to do all the work. His major role is finding work for everyone to do and helping them succeed in their calling.

One priority role of the church's ministry is highlighted in 1 Corinthians 12:13-16, that is, bringing believers to true maturity. This produces common understanding of doctrine, stability, effectiveness in ministry, and a climate in which each member of the body can properly function. Verse 16 is the key. When the congregation is truly united in the authority of Jesus and their love for one another, then each member (organ) of the body can effectively contribute that which God has ordained for him to do. When this happens, the body is healthy and just naturally grows in both numbers and Spirit.

Paul seems to indicate in Ephesians 4 the existence of two absolute essentials for church growth. First, a firm commitment that the Bible is the inspired, inerrant, revelation of both the message of salvation and the methods of evangelism. Second, we must truly fulfill Christ's new commandment to love *as* He loves. If these are present, a church can grow even if the principles of church growth are not understood (though knowledge of the principles may increase the growth). However, if either essential is missing, no amount of correct methodology will be effective.

If our motives are wrong, our product will be faulty. It is still His Kingdom, His power, and His glory!

2

Overcoming Hindrances to Growth

The worried parents measured Johnny against the kitchen wall. The yardstick confirmed their fears. He had stopped growing. Quickly they hurried Johnny to the doctor. "Make him grow, doctor," they said. "Give him a shot. Tell us what to do so we can get him growing again."

Now that is ludicrous. The doctor will not make him grow. Growth in a healthy young body occurs naturally. Instead, the doctor will attempt to find out what is not functioning properly.

Growth should be natural for a young, vital congregation. The important thing is not what we do to make a congregation grow; the important thing is to discover what is preventing growth.

When you ask leaders why their churches aren't growing, their answers center on facilities, finances, staff, or location. However, most barriers are not those which can be seen. These visible barriers are often the excuses that prevent leaders from analyzing and correcting the real barriers.

I once read that congregations grow easily to certain predictable plateaus. They will stay at those plateaus until they determine what they need to add, change, or delete. I went to our own Assemblies of God Sunday school statistics to see if these predicted plateaus do indeed occur. If certain growth principles were at work, then there would be large clusters of Sunday schools at certain attendance levels. And so it was—and is. These plateaus are at about 50, 90, 120, 180, 230, and 290 in average Sunday school attendance.

The theory of plateauing is that the congregation reaches some limit. It may be in the area of space, pastoral time, vision, desire, or organization. Once one of these barriers is identified and corrective measures taken, growth to the next plateau is usually quite rapid.

We can categorize these barriers as spiritual, mental, organizational, and physical. Let's explore them.

Spiritual Barriers

1. *Spiritual disease, senility, or death.* Some believe that congregations are predestined to patterns of infancy, vigorous youth, stable adulthood, middle-age lethargy, a golden period of warm memories, senility, and death. Now, it is true that individual churches sometimes die. Some of them have had glorious lives that deserve a beautiful memorial service before they are buried in the cemetery of history. But most dead churches are not buried. They are embalmed with tradition and ritual to give them the semblance of life.

But each of these three spiritual conditions has a solution. We can trust God for healing. Maybe we should pray as fervently for the health of the church as we do for the bodies of the saints. God grant that we guard His Body from injury and disease as we would our own.

If old age is evident, then pray for a renewal. The revival of the Spirit is indeed a church's fountain of youth.

If we find no vital signs left, we should have faith for at least a few resurrections. Granted, if the "patient" is kept breathing only because of an outside financial life-support system, then we need to consider pulling the plug and allowing it to gracefully die. But remember, with God all things are possible! Some of the greatest heroes of the faith were born of barren wombs. Isaac, Joseph, Samson, Samuel, and John the Baptist are not bad company with which to identify.

2. *Inadequate scriptural base.* Some attempt to interpret Scripture in a way to justify not growing. They place a low emphasis on evangelism. They begin to question

the authenticity and reliability of the Bible. This is soon followed by a humanistic effort to change society through social action programs.

The research of Dean Hoge in the book *Understanding Church Growth and Decline* shows strong correlation between conservatism in doctrine and church growth. That does not mean because a church is doctrinally correct that it will grow inspite of other barriers. But it is safe to observe that unless a solid scriptural foundation exists, a superstructure will not be built.

3. *Lack of prayer.* Prayer is our number one strategy against Satan. Prayer is spiritual warfare against the forces of evil. Through our communion with God, He quickens our minds and gives us the ability to see not only the needs of men but how to most effectively minister to those needs.

In the 1973 survey of our fastest growing Sunday schools, the pastors rated prayer as the number one priority. And the growing churches do not just talk about prayer— they pray! Every great revival in church history saw the truth of the Word flourish in the garden of prayer.

4. *The lack of faith that sees conditions as too difficult.* That premise denies Romans 5:20. Thank God that grace can still superabound where evil abounds! Jesus said the wheat and the tares would *grow together* until harvest. The same conditions that are ripening the tares for judgment are maturing the precious grain. Jesus said, "Lift up your eyes, and look on the fields; for they are white already to harvest" (John 4:35). The greatest moves of the Spirit always happen at the lowest ebbs of man's existence.

5. *Attempting to do it all ourselves, or expecting God to do it all.* How we vacilate between either of these two errors! We should not try to do what only God can do. Neither should we expect God to do what we can do. At Lazarus' tomb Jesus gave three commands. They form an outline of the church's responsibilities in reaching the person who is "dead in sins."

a. *"Take away the stone."* Jesus knew the people needed to be involved. He could have spoken to the rock and it would have moved aside. God can save men in spite of the stones of offense, prejudice, and hypocrisy. But we need to remove these barriers between men and God. Men put them there; men should remove them.

b. *"Lazarus, come forth."* We need to proclaim the salvation message in simplicity under the anointing of the Spirit. When we do, we can trust God for resurrection power.

c. *"Loose him, and let him go."* The church has a responsibility to provide nurture, fellowship, and training. It is not enough to bring a person to a decision. We must be willing to mature him into discipleship. Evangelism is not complete until we do so!

Mental Barriers

Today the 4-minute mile is commonplace. At one time men felt that barrier was unbreakable. However, Roger Bannister determined that his muscles could be conditioned to do it if his mind could believe it possible. And he did it. In breaking that mental barrier he made it possible for dozens of others to follow.

You will note that the grouping of mental barriers is the largest. Remember the Spirit has power to transform our minds so we can see with a spiritual eye instead of human vision.

1. *Inability to believe that God can use us.* Church growth is alright for Reverend So-and-so, but I don't have his personality or talents. God made each of us unique. Yet, few of us ever explore our potential.

Furthermore, we have too long confused humility with an inferiority complex. Humility is not a sense of worthlessness. It is being able to say with Paul, "I can do all things through Christ which strengtheneth me" (Philippians 4:13). When we have done something for God, we must admit that it was "Christ in me" and not my own abilities or strength.

2. *Traditionalism.* Churches attract tradition as ships attract barnacles. We follow the rut of the past instead of allowing the Spirit to sanctify our imaginations so that we might leap out of preconceived ideas and limits of human experience. Often we need only to break through the constraints of our traditional methods.

3. *Lack of vision.* The disciples saw a Samaritan woman and chided Jesus for breaking tradition. Jesus saw a harvest of souls.

Jesus once rebuked His disciples for their hardness of heart and unbelief. If He preached in your church would He do the same? We must see the true condition of men without Christ and believe that He will enable us to reach them.

Uncle Bud Robinson, colorful Nazarene preacher, was preaching at a lakeside camp. He began his sermon by telling how he had drowned an unwanted puppy in the lake.

"Folks," he said, "I didn't want to do it, but it had to be done. After I threw him in and commenced to row away he began to swim after me. I stopped rowing. The light of hope lit up his eyes, and he swam all the faster. Just when he got to the boat I rowed away again. I did that five or six times. Finally he began to slip beneath the surface.

"So I stopped the boat dead still. With his last feeble effort he tried to put his little paws over the edge of the boat and climb in, so I took an oar and began to beat his tiny little paws."

The audience listened in horror, wondering how a man of God could be so cruel.

He stood silent for several moments. Then he said, "Folks, I could go on telling this story about a puppy that never existed (except in my imagination) until you would all be in tears. But then I tell you that your friends and neighbors are going to a devil's hell, and you sit there dry-eyed blinking at me like Texas toads in a hailstorm."

That's a graphic illustration. Either we don't truly believe what the Bible teaches about the lost condition of men, or we are guilty of gross callousness.

4. *Projecting an exclusive image.* Millard Reed, in his excellent little book *Let Your Church Grow,* writes, "Most churches do not need to put signs on their lawns saying, 'Not welcome! Keep out!' They have already effectively communicated the message in many different ways."

One way this happens is for the church to become identified with one particular segment of the population. This may be a "family clan" where every one is interrelated. People outside the church see the only means of entry into the congregation as birth or marriage.

Often these churches have a family patriarch (or frequently a grandmother matriarch) who must approve people before God can add them to the church. These churches do not call a pastor, they adopt one.

A close identity with one cultural, social, or economic strata limits growth potential. If it is the "Transylvanian Assembly" then the community is told that unless they are a Transylvanian they will not likely be welcome. Or if the community sees the church as upper middle class, then the poor may well feel uncomfortable in attending.

A church's personality is either carefully and prayerfully developed by leadership or it will happen by default. Once an image is fixed in the minds of the community, you have limited yourself to the segment of the community you are likely to reach.

Family churches and ethnic churches often tend to be small because of limited exposure to fresh concepts. They often become inbred in their thinking.

5. *Unfriendliness.* In the previously mentioned survey of 1973's fastest growing Sunday schools, the pastors ranked only prayer and pastoral leadership as more essential to growth than friendliness. John Wimber, instructor of church growth at Fuller Theological Seminary and himself a successful pastor of a growing church, observes that most small churches have very thick skins. An outsider must be determined to break into the group.

Most people see themselves as friendly. They feel that
their congregation is open and warm. If they didn't they
wouldn't be a part of it. But what about the stranger? How
does he feel? In some churches the visitor feels he is intruding
into a family reunion.

Pastor Glen Cole, former pastor of Evergreen Christian
Center in Olympia, Washington, shared with me that the
turning point of their growth occurred when they began to
view everything they did through the eyes of the first-time
visitor. Their goal was for a visitor to feel like a long lost
member of the family arriving just in time for Thanksgiving
dinner.

One thing is certain: If you don't make a good first
impression you will not need to worry about making a second
impression.

6. *Self-satisfaction.* Some churches fear growth. They
can comfortably maintain ministries to their own families
and have respectability in the community. They feel that
growth will be at the sacrifice of the close fellowship they
enjoy. They give verbal priority to evangelism, but they are
not motivated to do more than that.

7. *Rose-colored rearview mirror.* The non-growing
church often remembers the past with myopic nostalgia.
Allegiance is invested in past leaders. New members are
often required to "mature" for several years before they are
permitted a place of ministry or leadership. (Research has
shown that leadership in growing churches includes many
who have been won to that church, while leadership in static
churches is predominantly those whose parents and grandparents were part of the same congregation.)

8. *No measurable goals.* Humans function best when
they have attainable goals which can be measured. Without
measurable success people become frustrated. *Frustrated* is
a word that describes too many Sunday schools and
churches. When success in reaching numerical goals is
thwarted, then unmeasurable goals are often substituted.
"We don't want quantity, we want quality. Spirituality is

more important than an increase in the number of class members."

That represents two errors in logic: First, God has not indicated that we must make a choice. Quantity and quality are not mutually exclusive. The church that becomes enamored with "how many" without paying attention to "how well" they minister will short-circuit God's plan. On the other hand, no Sunday school can claim it has quality ministry unless they are evangelizing the lost with measurable, visible results. To make such a claim while ignoring the Great Commission would be an admission that God's Word is being taught incorrectly. Both "how many" and "how well" are equally important.

The second error in the choice of quality over quantity is that qualitative goals are hard to measure. We want the church to be more spiritual, but how do we determine that? What criteria will you use to determine whether you have reached your goal?

Goals can be written in areas such as spiritual growth. We simply need to take the time to determine the kind of observable behavior that will indicate spiritual growth is occurring. If we fail to do this, without any supporting, visible evidence, we will rationalize that we have reached our goal. We must have some means for determining success in reaching goals.

9. *Demand for territorial rights or personal roles in the church.* This attitude can be characterized by the following comments which are heard far too often.

"Excuse me, you'll have to move. You're sitting in my pew!"

"I don't care if we have only five in this large classroom. This is our classroom. We paid for the paint."

"If I am not returned to the deacon board, then I will just have to find another church where I can fulfill my ministry."

How do you change such situations? We must prepare people for the changes that growth will require of us. But, we must also be gentle with those who associate personal memories of the past with certain places, and whose self-images are tied to the importance of their roles in the church.

Organizational Barriers

John Wimber observes that more churches are strangled by inadequate organizational patterns than are stymied by overcrowded facilities. It is important to keep in mind that organizational patterns must be constantly enlarged as the church grows. The strategies and policies that help you grow from the plateau of 65 to the plateau of 90 may keep you at 90 forever. Let's look at some of the organizational barriers that restrict growth.

1. *Forcing the pastor into an unscriptural role.* The pastor must be the leader. Peter Wagner, in *Your Church Can Grow,* writes that he would personally like to believe that the pastor is not the most essential person in the growth of the church. However, his research leads him to conclude the opposite. Growing churches are led by a man God is using to make it happen.

Here are some pastoral-people relationships that will hinder growth:

a. The pastor is subservient to the will of the people and/or board and must gain their approval before making any change or launching into new ministries.

b. The pastor is a hireling who becomes an "errand boy" for the parishioners.

c. The pastor is "paid," therefore he is responsible to do evangelism for the congregation.

2. *Inward focus.* A church that focuses most of its efforts, finances, and programming on meeting the needs of its own members soon ceases to evangelize. This inward focus is sometimes excused by claiming that nurture will produce evangelism. Win and Charles Arn, in their book, *Growth, A New Vision for the Sunday School,* state:

The belief that Sunday school growth will naturally result from personal growth and spiritual development of existing members is one of the primary reasons many Sunday schools today are declining. Such self-centered education *does not* motivate people toward involvement in the church's mission of growth and outreach. Education that concerns itself with only the spiritual nourishment of its own members contributes significantly to a 'self-service mentality' that effectively seals off the Sunday school from the outside world.

This was substantiated in a survey of the pastors of the 130 fastest growing Assemblies of God churches for the years 1973-78. These pastors gave high priority to evangelism in the Sunday school as well as recognizing its role to nurture and mature believers.

One way to determine if your school is inwardly focused is to evaluate how many programs, how much money, and how many workers are involved primarily in ministering to your own people versus how many are directed to reaching nonchurched people.

3. *Failure to create new units of ministry.* A unit is any cell, class, or group of your church that provides ministry to individuals. New classes and ministries normally grow the fastest. Merger of classes or ministries inevitably brings decrease. Growing churches are constantly expanding their contact points with the community.

4. *Building consciousness.* The fastest growing church in history had no building of its own. By using private homes for unit ministries and public facilities for high visibility rallies, the church in Jerusalem grew to about 5,000 adult male members within the first few months!

That ministry can happen only at a sacred place and time is a modern concept. The church is not a building erected at the corner of First and Vine. It is a holy temple being erected by God from "lively stones" scattered throughout the community.

We must go where people are. One thing is certain, if everything in your church happens within the church walls it can be safely predicted that not much is happening there either.

5. *Lack of priorities.* Something must be most important or nothing is important at all. Priorities must be established as to emphasis, effort, and sequence. What is the greatest goal? What deserves our greatest energies and budget? What must be done first?

Priorities keep us from wasting our resources. With our clearly established and well communicated priorities, we become like the little church where the ladies come every Wednesday afternoon to quilt and sew, so they will have nice things to sell in the fall bazaar, so they will have enough money to buy oil, so they have a nice warm place to come on Wednesday afternoons to quilt and sew, so they will have. . . . Let us be careful lest our operation is successful but the church dies!

6. *Perpetuation of nonproductive programs.* Churches have two great unwritten and unbreakable rules. Anything donated must be accepted, and once accepted, the item cannot be disposed of as long as one of the donor's descendants is still in the church.

Terminating a program is equally hard. We often confuse the sacredness and immutability of God's Word with our methods of propagating it. If a program was "given of God in response to Brother So-and-so's fasting and prayer," then we dare not change it. But to make method so sacred it cannot be changed is a subtle form of idolatry—worshiping the gift more than the Giver.

When Hezekiah discovered the people were burning sacred incense to Moses' brazen serpent, he broke it into pieces just as he had the images of Baal. He recognized that moving anything out of the time or purpose for which God ordains it is to make it a curse instead of a blessing.

But a word of caution before you start shooting the sacred cows. Remember, a fine line separates being revolutionary and being just plain revolting. Continuity must be in the midst of change. We must be able to bring "forth out of [our] treasure things new and old" (Matthew 13:52). We must blend the fresh and familiar.

Our Pentecostal pioneers were image breakers. Form, ritual, and tradition were fervently avoided. That permitted them to freely and creatively seek the leading of the Spirit and the truth of the Word to discover new methods of evangelism. They could be what God wanted in order to reach their generation. They knew the abiding principles, but they were innovative in particular matters. If they were alive today they would be on the cutting edge of what is happening in our generation.

Programs must be evaluated by their fruit. If an activity of the church is not producing results, then it does not deserve to channel personnel, time, budget, and energy from those ministries that are fruitful. Jesus offered only two alternatives for barren fig trees. Help it produce or cut it down.

Physical Barriers

These are relatively few, but they are still important.

1. *Appearance of buildings and grounds.* One of the first images people have of the church is of the building. A rundown building or unkept lawn communicates that the people who attend there really do not value their church. People also deduce that the church is not growing.

A common mistake of struggling churches is to spend what little money they can afford to improve the interior. Only the few who attend know that improvements have been made. The external appearance is also important. Paint, shrubs, flowers, and a manicured lawn cost little, but they tell the community that something is beginning to happen.

2. *Capacity of building and parking.* The eighty percent-of-capacity rule is still true. You will never *consistently* average the capacity of your facilities. Our American culture values personal space. Visitors resist having to walk all the way to the front or force their way into a pew that is already comfortably filled. More than enough space must be available if growth is to continue.

Many churches violate this principle. It is possible to overcrowd facilities for a limited period if you have genuine excitement, individuals are being ministered to, *and plans for the future exist,* but without facilities expansion, growth will ultimately stop.

If new facilities cannot be secured, additional space must be provided in innovative ways. Balancing the capacities of the auditorium and the Christian education facilities is also important. Remember, too, that sufficient parking space is vital in today's "shopping center" culture.

3. *Size of community.* Community size is not necessarily the same as the population of the city or area. As previously mentioned, the church can be identified with an ethnic group, socioeconomic strata, or other community within the larger population. These churches may need to enlarge their community by projecting a new identity to the city.

However, some churches located in towns, villages, and crossroads have no control over the community's population. Sometimes these pastors and churches become discouraged when they hear of super-sized churches in the urban areas. They feel as though they are running fast but standing still. They are reaching new people, but they only replace those who become infirm or die. The youth leave for college but never return because of economics.

One way to analyze growth in these situations is to figure the various avenues of growth or loss. To do this, take the names of those who have been added and removed from your Sunday school enrollment over the past few years. Then calculate those who

1. moved in minus those who moved away (migration gain/loss)

2. were born minus those who died (biological gain/ loss)

3. transferred from another church (transfer gain/loss)

4. were converted minus those whose lack of commitment led to their leaving the church (evangelism gain/loss)

If you are having biological and migration losses while gaining in evangelism, then you know you are doing some things right. Don't be discouraged and quit. Be aware that the limitations of the community's size may be more of a mental barrier than a physical one.

Here is a prayer to help prepare us for growth:

> O God, forgive us our pettiness and immaturity. Help us see that our goal must be to contribute to the Kingdom, rather than be concerned with what we can gain from it. Help us break through the barriers of our limited experience, preconceptions, and traditions. Teach us again to pray, and truly mean it, *Thine is the kingdom, and the power, and the glory, forever. Amen.*

3

Understanding What Makes
a Sunday School Grow

Why do some congregations grow rapidly while others remain static or decline? Is it because of circumstances over which they have control? Can a church choose to grow?

Four factors have been suggested as effecting the growth of churches. These are listed under the categories *contextual* and *institutional*. Contextual refers to circumstances, and institutional relates to the decisions and programs of the church.

The greatest influence on church growth is the sovereign will of God. The church is not controlled by sociological factors; it is a divine institution.

But contextual and institutional factors do influence the church. They can be either used, or overcome, in building a local congregation and Sunday school.

National Contextual

What happens in a particular time on the national scene provides either a positive or negative climate. Political, economic, and religious trends are important.

The last three presidents have all publicly testified to being "born again." The Moral Majority, the controversy over separation of church and state, and the electronic church have all contributed to a growing awareness of evangelical Christianity. Granted, not all the publicity has been positive, but at least people are aware of the church. The Church of Jesus Christ has prospered when it has had respect, and when it has been persecuted.

32

A recession may hinder funds for church expansion. Yet, historically, such times are characterized by increased conversions. People feel a need for God in trying times.

Local Contextual

A rapidly growing community provides not just more people, but more *reachable* people. People are more likely to change allegiance when they move into a new community. Social pressures in the nongrowing established community keep people loyal to the church of their tradition, even if their spiritual needs are not met or their attendance is hit-or-miss.

The area's economy affects the church. In smaller rural areas young people often must leave to find employment. The opening of a new industry may bring an influx of people who, already evangelized, identify with the church. Another local congregation may reject the testimony of their charismatic members. Sometimes a local Assembly receives a windfall of growth. Other Assemblies may feel that they are struggling to replace members who move.

National Institutional

Local churches seldom grow as a direct result of decisions made at the national level. However, the national headquarters must provide an emphasis that gives direction for growth. It can also offer guidance, helps, programs, and training.

Although national leadership is vital, the work of growing a church is done by the local church itself. Let me illustrate.

The Assemblies of God has an effective national leadership base for church growth. Let us reemphasize those things which the Spirit, through national leaders, has provided.

First, we have an unshaken commitment to the Scriptures. Peter Wagner, in a private conversation at the 1978 Council on Church Growth conducted in Kansas City, commented how refreshing it was to be with a group whom he didn't have to constantly remind that the Bible is God's Word. The Assemblies of God have always maintained that Scriptures are reliable and trustworthy because they are fully inspired. The Bible not only tells us what God wants the church to do, but also how to do it.

Second, we have a clearly defined purpose. At the 1968 Council on Evangelism we defined our reasons for being:

1. Ministry to God in worship;
2. Ministry to fellow believers in fellowship, education, and spiritual growth;
3. Ministry to unbelievers through evangelism. Growing churches understand this purpose and keep a healthy blend of these three areas of ministry.

Third, we have a commitment to growth. We believe that God wants every person in every nation to hear the gospel and respond positively to it. Historically, a major evaluation of a pastor's leadership and a congregation's health has been numerical growth. We have had a pragmatism that has kept us from substituting dialogue for effective ministry. Although not every means can be justified by its end result, no means or methods can be justified if they do not produce measurable results.

Fourth, a Scriptural understanding of the interaction of the Holy Spirit and the Inspired Word. We believe that the Bible is complete. But we also understand and take seriously the continuing activity of the Holy Spirit in the world. He convicts of sin; He empowers believers; He guides into truth. He reveals God's will in areas that Scripture does not detail.

We have always contended for an interaction of doctrine and experience, for both are important. We must know both the Scriptures and the power of God. But doctrine and experience must agree. However, the test of human experience is the revealed Word, not vice-versa.

Fifth, a unique blend of local church sovereignty and voluntary cooperation in both district and general councils.

Our founders, through the genius of the Holy Spirit, wed the dynamics of congregationalism with the stability of presbyterian forms of church government.

We are united in matters of doctrine, morality, cooperative efforts in missions, and Christian fellowship. Yet each Assembly has the freedom to find God's specific directions for its own situation. It is free to be, and to become, what it needs to be in order to effectively minister to its community. We have maintained unity without demanding a stifling uniformity.

Local Institutional

At the Association of Statisticians of American Religious Bodies' annual meeting in 1979, Dr. Dean Hoge shared a brilliant analysis of church membership trends and the four factors of growth. A marked division in the attitude of the attending denominational leaders followed. The mainline denominational leaders felt that the national contextual conditions were contributing to their declines in membership. Some even took comfort in the findings of Dr. Hoge's research.

But the evangelical leaders felt that what was happening in national circumstances was not the most important of the four factors. They felt that what the local church, under God's direction, chose to do was the secret of why their churches were growing. As mentioned previously, the Assemblies of God has always placed strong emphasis upon the local church.

What, then, are the earmarks of the growing congregations? What separates them from nongrowing churches? Although you may not find all of the following features in every growing church, you will find a majority in each of them.

1. *A firm faith that their church can grow.* Instead of a "not now," "not here," or "not me" attitude, the congregation of a growing church believes that God will use them in their unique situation.

They believe that they have, or God will give them, everything they need to see their church advance. They understand that only God can give the increase. They don't attempt to do what only God can do, neither do they demand God to do what He has assigned to them as members of His Church.

They have a pastor who knows that he is divinely called and that he has the plan of God for the situation. The pastor and people enjoy a good relationship. The congregation genuinely responds to his leadership.

2. *Spiritual worship*. The services exhibit an excitement. The people enjoy going to church. The style of worship varies because the congregation understands that cultural differences influence how we express ourselves to God. Nevertheless, adoration and spontaneous worship to the Lord remains constant. Music is appropriate to the tastes of the people and is easy to sing. All elements of the worship service usually focus on a central theme. However, the Spirit is free to move in the hearts of the people.

Worship is the church's first priority. The congregation realizes that they must properly relate to God if they are to be useful in evangelism.

Jesus is altogether lovely. A church that extols Christ in worship is an attractive church. A church that learns to truly worship God will grow, unless they fail to balance ministry to God with ministry to the believers and evangelization of the lost. Balance is the key word.

3. *Belief in the active power of God*. A spiritual expectancy is present among them. They trust God to supply needs for both individuals and the corporate body of believers. They pray for the sick, and expect God to confirm His Word by His active involvement in their lives. They seek to be used by the Holy Spirit according to the gifts He provides.

4. *Sanctified imagination*. The ability to dream and plan is part of the Godlike image of man. What the Spirit allows us in faith to believe we can do for God, He will

empower us to accomplish. We must learn to be visionary people, for without a vision, we will perish.

5. *Making ways instead of excuses.* Growing churches innovate. When barriers of limited facilities, lack of workers, or past traditions block their progress, they *find* a way to provide ministry. Instead of saying, "We cannot grow because . . .," they declare, "We must find a way to continue to minister to the needs of people."

Innovation is the ability to break out of old molds of thinking, scheduling, and methodology. It means moving beyond the restraints of previous experience in order to do things differently. The Word of God is unchanging. Our goal of ministry should not vary. But, we need to be flexible enough to change how we do things—especially if they are not productive.

For example, a traditional pattern of ministering viewed Sunday morning as the time to speak to the church and Sunday evening as the time to be evangelistic. That used to work. Then came TV, and its prime time—the evening. It took many of us years to realize that we had to evangelize on Sunday morning when unconverted people are most likely to visit our services.

Copying someone else's innovation is not being innovative. Failure can occur when one church tries to duplicate the programs of another. Circumstances vary; communities are different; the skills and gifts of the people are not the same in every church.

We should be aware of the methods of successful churches. But we should be investigators, not imitators. We must learn to adapt methods to our own circumstances.

We need also to permit the Holy Spirit to show us new ways of accomplishing our spiritual goals. All the good ideas have not yet been born. Why not seek God to creatively inspire you and your church in ways to enlarge His kingdom in your community?

6. *An effective blend of evangelism methods.* The farmer diversifies his crops because he knows that

conditions may vary from season to season. Likewise the growing church does not put all of its energy into one outreach effort. It recognizes the need for several avenues of evangelism: a balance of such activities within and without the church facilities, a blend of individual and corporate execution.

7. *Ministries tailored to community needs.* Growth occurs when the needs of people are being met. The greatest need of man is a right relationship with God. From this vital communion flows the supply of other needs. But most unconverted people do not understand this.

Jesus said we should not offer pearls to swine. Why? Think for a moment what would happen if the farmer dumped pearls into the hog trough. The hogs *felt* need would be hunger. They would try to eat the pearls. When they found them hard and tasteless, they would trample them underfoot. They wouldn't realize the value of the pearls.

So it is with those who have no spiritual insight. We have to translate our pearls into love, acceptance, and meeting their needs. As we meet their felt needs, we can lead people to understand their deeper spiritual needs. We must never allow ministry to people's physical and emotional needs, as important as they are, to become an end in itself. Our ultimate goal is to see lives changed through the redemptive power of God.

8. *Open doors and open hearts.* Growing churches are easy to get into. They have many "doors." Peter Wagner observes that most evangelical churches used to be "side door" churches, meaning their first contact with outsiders was in an auxiliary ministry. We claimed that Sunday school was the greatest evangelistic arm of the church. That used to be true. Today, however, it is easier to attract people to the worship service, our "front door."

This does not mean we do not need our departmental and educational ministries. Discipleship occurs best in small groups. But we need to understand the principle of keeping as many "doors" open to the church as we can.

Growing churches have open hearts, as well as open doors. They love people and make it easy for them to become part of the group. They consciously structure their buildings, ministries, and even positions of leadership and Christian service so that people do not have to force their way into the church.

9. *Utilitarian buildings.* There are some exceptions, but generally the growing church does not have a facility like a cathedral. The edifice is not a monument to past glories. It is the barracks for a growing army of God's people. Facilities are planned with multiple uses in mind. Classrooms are large to accommodate classes with multiple teachers and workers.

10. *High visibility in the community.* Visibility is the complement of vision. Vision is our ability to see the people who need to be reached. Visibility is the ability of the church to be seen by those people and identified as a place where they can receive help. No one will come to a church he doesn't know exists.

A lovely edifice on the interstate highway can provide visibility. But growing churches increase the communities awareness of their ministries in a number of ways.

11. *Constant enlargement of ministry and staff.* Every believer is a priest who can intercede with God. Every Christian can be empowered to share the gospel. But, growing churches do more than challenge people to get involved. They also provide opportunities for training and practical on-the-job supervision. Just as it is easy to become a member of the body of believers of a growing church, it is easy to become a worker. Growing churches are enabling churches. They help people find a place of service and provide both training and tools.

12. *Focus on responsive groups of people.* You discover that growing churches have identified people and areas of the community that are likely to be responsive to the church's outreach efforts to them. Usually this group of people will be similar to those who are already part of the

church. The homogenous unit principle of church growth says that churches grow best when they attempt to reach people who are similar to them in culture. This principle is demonstrable. However, it is no excuse for a church to be racially, culturally, or economically segregated.

The homogenous unit principle relates to how people are won to the Kingdom, not what the church should be in either fellowship or worship. We all feel most comfortable with those who share similar values, philosophies, and life-styles. If a person must cross a cultural barrier, even a small one, he is less likely to come into the church. This is why we need to carefully select the image we project. Once an image of the church is fixed in the minds of the community, it limits the segment of the community the church is likely to reach. We must not allow that circle to be drawn too small.

Growing churches add ministries to attract and minister across cultural barriers, but it is more effective to adapt our methods to fit the culture instead of making the culture become like us in order to be a part of the church.

13. *Structure for growth.* Growing churches recognize the need for constantly evaluating their organizational patterns and making necessary changes that will permit further growth. They have a healthy blend of outreach and maintenance ministries. They are structured so that the threefold purpose of worship, spiritual growth, and evangelization can best occur.

Peter Wagner, in his book *Your Church Can Grow* defines the three size groupings in the church that best permit these ministries to occur: (1) cells, (2) congregations, and (3) celebration.

Cells are small, usually 6 to 10 persons. They permit close fellowship and a nonthreatening atmosphere in which needs can be shared and met. Accountability to others functions best in the cell. The extreme limit of cell size is about 20 persons. Some churches are single celled. They do not want to grow beyond the size where cell ministries occur.

The way to grow is to divide the cell in order to multiply. As one pastor of a growing church expressed it, "We decided if we were going to grow larger we had to grow smaller by providing many cell ministries."

Congregations are usually 25 to 100 persons, and each person knows the others by first name and occupation. In most large churches the adult Sunday school classes provide the aspects of congregational ministry. Each congregation will usually be homogenous in age, needs, and culture patterns. To grow beyond 100, a church must recognize the need for, and provide, multiple congregations. This does not mean a church split, though giving *birth* to a new church may be just what God desires.

Celebration is the church in worship. Here there is no limiting size. To effectively worship God you do not need to speak the same language as the person next to you or even know his name. But celebration alone cannot build a strong, stable church. Without the functions of the cell and congregational groupings, little nurture of converts, training of leaders, or commitment to meet the needs of fellow believers will occur.

Traditionally the Sunday school provided these things. It allowed each individual to be ministered to at his or her particular point of need. Follow-up of prospects and absentees could be easily accomplished because of the small group structures. Sunday school provided constant opportunities for new leaders to develop.

We do not need to force Christian education into limited concepts of our past experience, but we should be careful about moving from the proven success and values of a properly organized Sunday school.

14. *Acceptance of new challenges and situations.* Jesus said the fruitful branches would be purged. This has been viewed as a purifying process. However, the vinedresser prunes the vines to force new growth—and new growth produces fruit. Growth in leadership, structure, and people must happen if we are to be fruitful.

4

The Components of a Growth Strategy

Leaving the Chariton, Iowa, hospital where my father was a patient, I remembered a shortcut just north of town that would take me to Interstate 35. I got in my car and drove slowly north. Finally, I realized I had missed the turnoff. I drove back to town. Just as I arrived at the city limit I realized that Chariton isn't even close to the interstate highway. I was thinking about Osceola!

I had proved a well-known point—You can't get there from here if you don't know where "here" is. Evaluation must come before goal setting and planning. In Luke 14:25-33 Jesus taught about the cost of discipleship. Both the tower builder and the army general needed to evaluate what they had to work with before they set a goal they could not accomplish. This is true in building a congregation.

We must know our strengths, weaknesses, assets, and potentials. Then, these things must be yielded to God. It is not what we are, or what we have, but what He can do with what we put at His disposal.

We can grow if we want to. Most churches have sufficient time, workers, finances, and opportunities to grow, even if in a limited way. You may not agree with that statement. Granted, you may not have enough to grow to a congregation of 1,000. But that isn't the first goal. As a congregation reaches each level of growth, they will discover that they have the ability to grow to the next level. A strategy for growth is required.

This strategy involves four steps: (1) evaluate where you

are; (2) determine where you want to go; (3) plan how to get there; and (4) implement your plans. The cycle of success both begins and ends with evaluation. Evaluation is necessary to help us set attainable goals, and the basis of developing plans since it reveals what we have to work with.

Good goals always define how much, how far, and how soon. And we must set a date for evaluating whether we have reached the goal. If we have, then we simply set new goals based on our reevaluation of the situation.

If the goal has not been reached, then we must evaluate whether the original goal was reasonable, our plans were inadequate, or whether they were properly carried out. The cycle of success, like a bicycle, works best when it is in motion: It is easier to keep your balance and momentum.

What are the areas that a local congregation needs to evaluate? What tools and methods are available to help us discover where "here" is?

People

A church's greatest asset is its people. Although God has the power to build the Church without our help, He has chosen to use men and women. Therefore, we need to understand our people.

The concentric circles of growth diagram on page 44 will help you visualize the various "people pools" in your congregation. Think of your congregation as spheres inside of each other instead of pools. Visualize a number of balloons, each slightly smaller than the one it is in.

If one balloon continues to be inflated, it will become as large as the one surrounding it. Then one of three things will occur. It may burst the next balloon and keep growing. It may push the other balloon, making it even larger. Or, if the larger balloon is strong enough, the smaller balloon (i.e., growth) will be stopped no matter how hard you blow! It is much the same with the various groupings of people in a congregation. Evaluating the size relationships of the various pools, or spheres, will help you discover what needs to be done to promote further growth.

CONCENTRIC CIRCLES OF GROWTH

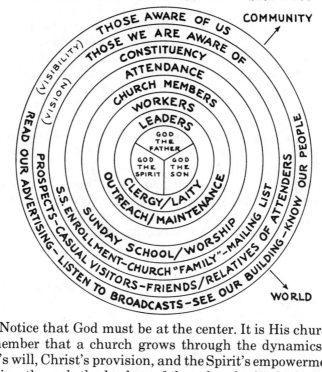

Notice that God must be at the center. It is His church. Remember that a church grows through the dynamics of God's will, Christ's provision, and the Spirit's empowerment flowing through the leaders of that church. As the leaders' administrative gifts function, the church will grow.

The previous paragraph describes the first theory of how concentric circles grow. That is, the force of growth comes from within. The Spirit reveals God's plans for growth and guides the leaders in implementing what God desires to be done. As this force is present, the church naturally grows.

The second theory we might call the vacuum principle. As each circle enlarges, it tends to pull the next circle along with it. Enrollment grows and attendance follows. Membership increases, as does the reservoir of workers and leaders. If the church increases its visibility, the number of prospects will proportionately follow.

Which of the two theories is correct? Perhaps they are not conflicting theories at all, but complementary. The growth that comes through leaders empowered by the Spirit is essential. But that growth can be stalled if proper attention is not given to each of the growth rings. When the church is healthy it grows through the ministry of the people.

Mathematically calculate the relationship between the number of persons in each of the concentric rings. What is the ratio of full-time paid staff to worship attendance? In most Assemblies of God churches the ratio is 150 to 200 in attendance for each full-time salaried staff member. Few pastors have the ability to lead a church in growth above 250 in attendance without adding additional ministerial staff. They simply run out of time. If the church is to continue to grow, more leadership must be provided. As a multiple staff is built, each minister can develop his special skills and calling. This increases efficiency.

However, hiring additional staff is not the only answer. Too often it is easier to pay someone to do what lay leadership should be trained to do. A proper ratio of leadership should exist between clergy and laity.

One of the most important ratios to watch is that of workers to Sunday school enrollment. National figures for our Assemblies of God Sunday schools, charted for nearly 40 years, show that when enrollment increases proportionately faster than the number of teachers and officers, growth slows or levels off. Likewise, each of the great periods of Sunday school growth has been preceded by an increase in the number of workers.

Depending on the size of the school's enrollment, a ratio of 6 to 10 members to each teacher is healthy. A smaller school will have a higher ratio of workers since their classes, if properly graded, will be smaller. Also, a school with 40 enrolled and 4 general officers will have a 10 to 1 ratio without a teaching staff.

Another ratio to determine is the number involved in maintenance ministries (those directed to the needs of the congregation) to the number engaged in evangelism and outreach. Both groups are necessary for growth, but they must be in balance.

The relationship of church membership to attendance is vital. We must bring people into a commitment to support the body of Christ with their time, talent, and tithe. We should attempt to bring every believer into membership.

But we must guard against membership becoming a substitute for salvation or commitment. Our Assemblies of God churches have traditionally had much larger attendances than membership. This reveals that our members are active in the life of the church. It is interesting to note that not one A/G congregation appears among the 100 largest churches in America ranked according to membership in *The Complete Book of Church Growth.* However, 15 to 20 A/G churches are in each of the three categories ranked according to worship attendance, Sunday school attendance, and total giving.

A powerful statistic to watch is the ratio of Sunday school attendance to enrollment. Again, analysis of our four decades of national statistics reveal that when attendance increases faster than enrollment, growth slows dramatically. When enrollment increases proportionately, growth continues.

This Active Participation Rate (APR) is calculated by dividing average weekly attendance by total enrollment. For instance, if you average 100 in attendance and have an enrollment of 150, you have an APR of 67 percent. Contrary to popularly held opinion, 100 percent in attendance is not only a difficult goal to attain, it is unhealthy. A good ratio for most churches (smaller rural schools will likely have a higher APR) is 50 to 60 percent.

If your APR is over 60 percent it will likely indicate that you need to emphasize outreach. Or, it may be that you have a restrictive policy of enrollment which keeps new persons from being quickly added to the role. Or, it may be that casual attenders are prematurely removed.

On the other hand, an APR lower than 50 percent may indicate a need to improve your Sunday school ministries and methods of follow-up. An unusually low APR, in either the total attendance or a department or class may be the result of overcrowding the facilities.

Watch the relationship of Sunday school attendance to morning worship attendance. In most churches today Sunday school is falling behind. The question of the 50s was, "How do we get them to stay for church?" Now it is, "How do we get them to come for Sunday school?" The Bible shows the need for a balance between worship and the study of the Word (Spirit and truth), that is, knowing the power of God and knowing the Scriptures. Convincing evidences from other denominations indicate that a deemphasis in Christian education produces future declines in membership and attendance. Sunday school is not a "department" of the church—*it is the church* in corporate study of God's Word!

The outer two rings of the concentric circles are difficult to measure. But they are very important. The growing church is continually increasing its list of prospects. We must constantly be alert for those who are most likely to respond to the ministries we provide. The "those we are aware of" pool is a result of our people's vision.

The outer ring represents our visibility. If you desire to analyze your community's awareness of your church, you may want to do a simple survey of a randomly selected sample. You might go to every fifth house in a given section of the city and ask them if they are aware of your church and where it is located. You might also want to ask a few simple questions that would reveal what image the community has of the church and its beliefs.

Notice that each ring of people is built out of the one just beyond. If you discover a ring that is almost as large as the one outside it, you will know where you need to give special attention.

Your present constituency may be analyzed in other interesting and vital ways. What percentage were "born" into the church, that is, their parents were attending the church when they were born? How many were already born again when they first started attending? Are large segments of the congregation interrelated by either birth or marriage?

High percentages in any of the above categories usually indicate a congregation that is oriented toward maintenance. They focus inward on their own needs and desires.

Is your church representative of the community in age, race, economy, and cultural mix? We will look at community analysis later, but keep in mind that if your church is not reaching a particular segment of the community, you must plan ways to reach them. One good way is to start another Assembly with ministries geared to their needs.

Image

A poet once wrote, "Oh, to be able to see ourselves as others see us." Perhaps we need to survey people in the community to discover what they know about the church. How do they see you doctrinally? Are you friendly? Do you project a growth image? Is your church exclusive? Remember that it is our responsibility to communicate who we are. If we discover a negative image in the community, we need to correct it.

It would be wise to conduct the same survey of your own people. If you discover a widely divergent opinion between the community and the church, you need to get busy.

Potential Worker Survey

At least once a year conduct an interest/experience/ skills survey of your congregation. The national Sunday School Department, 1445 Boonville, Springfield, MO 65802, can supply two different surveys for your use. Even in small congregations such a survey will reveal abilities and skills which the leaders did not know. Information from the survey and a plan for evenly employing the potential workers should be shared with the leaders of all departments.

Finances

In many congregations all money is spent in maintaining the already established ministries. Little, if any, is spent in evangelism and outreach. Especially in the nongrowing congregations attention must be given to establishing proper priorities on expenditures.

List all expenditures, and divide them into two categories: ministries to the church, and ministries in evangelism. If you begin to spend a lot of time debating whether a particular item is maintenance or outreach, that indicates you are too oriented toward maintenance.

Do not include any contributions to ministries outside your community such as foreign missions or district support. These are vital. But do not use them to compensate for failure to sponsor a local outreach to your community.

Facilities

Start by looking at the exterior of the building. Is it attractive and in good repair? Is the lawn neatly mowed? Are you proud of the way your building represents you to those who pass by?

Walk through your church. Does the foyer say "welcome" when you walk in? Are there signs to guide visitors toward the appropriate classes? Are the floors clean? Do the restrooms smell pleasant? Would you like your baby to be left in the nursery room? Are the classrooms neat and attractive? Are they light and airy? Are the decorations attractive and periodically changed?

Remember that you tend to bias your evaluation of the facilities since you are use to seeing them as they usually are. Our own clutter never looks as bad as someone else's.

Needs for space are easily observed. However, we often make common mistakes in evaluating the need to provide more room. Many feel no need for expansion as long as there is room for one more. This is demonstrably a false notion.

Arthur Flake, head of the Southern Baptist Sunday

School Board in the 1920s, devised a number of growth laws. He discovered that when a department is consistently running 80 percent of capacity, growth stalls. This 80 percent rule also relates to the auditorium seating. "More than enough" space must be available if a church is to continue to grow.

Using the space requirements suggested by the national Sunday School Department figure the optimum capacity of each classroom. Compare the total capacity of the Christian Education facilities with the seating capacity of the auditorium. They should be in fairly close balance. Also compare these figures with the number of parking spaces available. You should have at least one parking space for every three persons your facilities can handle.

Organization

You should have a written policy of operation that guides the Sunday school. It should be updated about every two years. Measure its effectiveness by asking, "Is it being followed or ignored?" Have you communicated your Sunday school policies to all workers? Be sure to provide written job descriptions for all staff members.

Who has the responsibility to recruit workers for the Sunday school? Do you have a clearly understood strategy for making selections and providing training? You should have some means for continuing evaluation of a workers efficiency. Consider the necessity of providing enrichment opportunities for the present staff. Also, be sure funds are budgeted to help workers improve their ministries.

Visitors

How do you identify visitors? Do you recognize first-time visitors in a manner that makes them feel important without embarrassing them? What kind of follow-up is used? Do you keep records of visitors who are prospects (as contrasted with visitors who are members of another church who may visit some special service)? What percentage of these prospects return a second time? How many become regular attenders?

A limited number of visitors indicates a need to increase your visibility and outreach efforts. However, if you have many visitors but have a low return rate, you may want to reevaluate your ministries. You may not have been prepared to minister to their needs.

We should also keep records and carefully evaluate conversions. What percentage of persons making a first-time commitment to Christ become part of your church? If your retention rate is low, what plan of follow-up and ministry do you have for new converts? Have you trained altar workers?

Friendliness

How do people get into your church? Where are the doors? We are not speaking of the doors of the building, but rather the doors into the body of believers. If, while surveying your people, you discover most of them were born into the church, you have already concluded that you must make new efforts for reaching people.

If you have people who recently came into the church, ask what attracted them. You will likely discover that the vast majority became part of the body because some person was their "door" and helped them into the congregational life.

Another way to evaluate how people come into your church is to determine what program or person motivated new persons to enroll in the Sunday school during the past year.

Community

You will want to become thoroughly acquainted with your community and its needs. The secret of growth is to wed the gifts and ministries of your church with the needs of the community.

What other churches are ministering in your area? Which of them do you consider to be evangelical? If you do not have good access to the religious statistics of your county, you may write the office of the Assemblies of God Statistician, 1445 Boonville, Springfield, MO 65802. The statistician can supply you with detailed statistics on the various religious bodies in your county and total membership figures for each denominational group.

Your local library should have a copy of the *Statistical Abstract of the United States.* This book will show you figures on births, marriages, divorces, income levels, age/sex/race ratios, and other valuable information about your county. These may help you discover groups of people who are not being ministered to by any church. Your Chamber of Commerce can also supply you with data.

The U.S. Census Bureau publishes an atlas for each major metropolitan area. It can be obtained from the United States Commerce Department Office in most major cities. The atlas shows major demographic characteristics of each census tract. This is valuable in planning ministries and seeing the potential for new church planting.

Check with local utility companies or Welcome Wagon International to obtain the names of newcomers in the community.

Understand the cultural patterns of the community. Remember, people are easier to reach if we do not make them change cultural patterns. We must be willing, as Paul was, to adapt ourselves to their culture in order to reach them.

Ministries

List the varied ministries of your church. How many are primarily for church members and which are outreach in emphasis. Which are producing results and which aren't? Which do you need to terminate? Which deserve more effort and investment? What needs to be added to these ministries?

Evaluation

You may be thinking, *He wants us to evaluate everything!* Evaluation is important and we must be careful that evaluation is honest and not used in an attempt to support preconceived conclusions. Also, we must avoid morbid introspection. We must turn our eyes to the "Author and Finisher of our Faith." Regardless of our abilities or inabilities, assets or liabilities, strengths or weaknesses, God will empower us to build the Church if we will listen to His Word and His Spirit.

5

Developing a Growth Strategy for Your Church

As a young boy, I hated to gather eggs in the spring. The same natural forces that caused the crocuses to blossom stirred maternal instinct in the hens. No longer did they view an egg as a day's work. They were instead progeny to be protected with beak and claw.

Because brooding hens cease laying, mother would shut them in the coop. Obstinate ones got a special treatment. Mother would place them on a nest of china eggs. Eventually the hen would grow weary of trying to hatch those beauties and go back to laying. If not, we had chicken and noodles.

How many times have we worked hard, prayed for God's blessing, and became frustrated because our plans were unhatchable? Wouldn't it be better to discover the plans already blessed of God?

In their 1966 book *Latin American Church Growth*, Read, Monterroso, and Johnson stated that the Pentecostal churches of Latin America were growing because they were using effective methods of evangelism and church growth. "The genius of the Pentecostals," they wrote, "is to be free to find new methods."

In *Look Out, the Pentecostals are Coming* (republished as *What Have We Been Missing*), Peter Wagner arrived at the same conclusion. Pentecostal churches were not growing simply because they were "Pentecostal," but because they had discovered effective methods.

From where did those effective methods come? They were discovered as a result of studying the Scripture and following the leading of the Holy Spirit. Only as our human minds are quickened by the Spirit do we become truly creative in our planning.

While dedication and commitment cannot make ineffective strategies effective, neither will good methods accomplish our goals without committed and motivated Christians to use them. Methods do not work—workers work!

Your strategy of church growth is vital. It must be born by touching the mind of God. He has a blueprint for your church, and He wants to reveal it to you.

No one can devise the proper plan for your church. That is your responsibility as a leader of the congregation. Here are some suggestions you should take as you plan your strategies.

Study the Scriptures

The Bible tells us that God wants the church to grow, and it reveals the ways growth occurs. Scripture contains three major allegories for the church. Each of them gives us insight in how the church is built.

First Corinthians 12, Ephesians 4, and Romans 12 all tell us that the church grows like a body. When that body is healthy, it edifies itself by ingesting new people into the fellowship and assimilating them into the body to create new cells and organs. The major organs for growth are the digestive system.

In 1 Corinthians 3:1-9, Paul compares the Corinthian church to a farm where he and Apollos have been placed to assist God in producing a harvest. The various roles of planting, cultivating, irrigating, and harvesting are all vital. But, it is God who causes the seed to grow and produce fruit.

The basic principle is that the seed (God's Word) must be sown in the hearts of receptive people. When the seed sprouts and grows, it needs to be cultivated until harvest. The same is true in church growth. We have not really produced a disciple until he has been nurtured to maturity and produces fruit for the kingdom.

First Corinthians 3:10-12, Ephesians 2:20-22, and 1 Peter 2:4-8 all compare the Church to a building. God is taking "lively stones" and mortaring them together with love and Christian fellowship. When we permit Him to place us where He desires, this building becomes a glorious temple inhabited by God.

Each allegory gives us insights into how God is causing the Church to grow and how we can best be used to assist His work. Study the Scriptures. We gain necessary wisdom from them for our own salvation and the salvation of others.

Pray

As previously mentioned, the pastors in the 1973 survey of fast-growing churches rated prayer as the most indispensable factor in growth.

In preaching to his own congregation on Sunday morning, January 2, 1983, pastor Arvid Kingsriter reminded the members of First Assembly in Bloomington, Minnesota, that "every ministry must be based on prayer." This steadily growing congregation has traditionally observed the first week of each year as a time of fasting and intense prayer. Founded in 1954, its current attendance is approaching 1,000.

One of the most rapidly growing churches of the 80s has been First Assembly of God in Grand Rapids, Michigan. They have grown from 450 in 1977 to an average attendance of 3000 in 1982. Pastor Wayne Benson, writing in the December 6, 1982, edition of *Lamb Light,* the church's official publication, reflected on God's leading. He wrote that in early 1982,

> God, through His Word, directed us to cease all of our normal activities. The wheels of ministry came to a grinding halt; all of the machinery was quieted so we could *listen.* Isaiah 55 became precious to us during those days. "Ho! Everyone who is thirsty come to the waters." (Isaiah 55:1). We felt impressed to call a period of prayer and fasting which involved our whole congregation.

We had to have a new revelation. We needed a new dynamic from which we could draw fresh water. We were given a new set of demands from the Holy Spirit as a direct result. Second, the inertia of ministry had become like a freight train. We had to stop where we were and rest in the Spirit. We needed to drink from God's waters of revelation and power. We needed to get a fix upon a brand new vision.

General plans for church growth are clearly revealed in Scripture, but we need prayer and the communion of the Spirit to quicken our minds to see what the Scriptures are saying. We also need to determine the particulars of God's plans for our own situation. As promised in Romans 8:26, 27, the Spirit assists our prayers and helps us to determine God's will.

Prayer and communion with God are the source of our motivation and strength. Paul told the Galatians that we are absolutely certain of reaping the harvest unless we become weary in well doing or faint (Galatians 6:9). "But they that wait upon the Lord shall renew their strength; they shall mount up with wings as eagles; they shall run, and *not be weary;* and they shall walk and *not faint.*" (Isaiah 40:31).

Building a Faith That the Church Can Grow

A vital interaction must occur between pastor and people if the church is to have faith to grow. The pastor must be certain of his call. Out of this confidence that he is God's man in God's place comes an ability to transmit his vision to the people. It also makes him credible in the eyes of the congregation. Their confidence in God becomes a certainty that He will use them to help His church grow.

A "can-do" attitude must be created. Only then will the people really have a vision of what God wants them to do and a belief that they can accomplish it.

Paradoxically, before success comes, a willingness to fail must be present, that is, a climate where people are free to adventure in the Lord without everyone saying, when success is not immediate, "I told you it wouldn't work." The

Parable of the Talents tells us that the greatest failure of all is to be so afraid of failing that we do nothing.

Another important factor in developing a belief that God "can do it with us" is exposure to growing churches. The people should be encouraged to visit growing churches when they vacation. The pastor needs to learn from others whose churches are growing. Church growth books and stories of growing congregations are invaluable. The bibliography at the back of this book contains many excellent titles.

It is also imperative that early goals of growth are attained. Nothing fuels faith for growth like growth itself.

Emphasize Worship

Spiritual worship will attract people to our churches. Be sure freedom and vitality characterizes the worship services. They must be structured to permit time for adoration of God and the moving of the Holy Spirit. The congregational music in most of our growing churches is Scripture and worship choruses that help people to express praise to God. A time of ministry to those who are physically or spiritually hurting is usually included. Everything centers around a worship theme culminating in the proclamation of the Word and an opportunity for response.

Dream

Staff and other leadership teams must schedule times when they can collectively share their dreams and plans for the church in a visionary way. Group planning permits all of the leaders to feel that the plans are "theirs." This will increase their motivation to see their vision fulfilled.

Remember that these brainstorming times are for a free-wheeling sharing of ideas and dreams. No evaluation should be done at this stage. It is a time for "getting it down." "Getting it good" comes later. Do not permit anyone to say, "We tried it once and it didn't work."

Schedule periodic times of breakaway for the leaders of the various ministries of the church. This can be as simple as an afternoon or evening (removed from the telephone) or as involved as a two-day planning meeting in a retreat setting. These need to be times of evaluating progress, setting goals, and making plans. They must also be times of prayer and seeking the mind of God.

Identify Community Needs

The Parable of the Sower tells us that we need to sow the seed where it will bring the greatest harvest. We need to target our efforts for those who are most likely to respond.

Responsive groups can often be identified by evaluating those who are already being won. You may discover a particular age or cultural group in the community to whom you need to give special attention. An evaluation of where your people live may also show you that a certain section of the community is particularly receptive to the gospel.

Community analysis may also reveal pockets of need. Some of the groups you discover are not being adequately ministered to by any church. These may include the poor, migrant workers, ethnic minorities, children of unchurched parents, divorced, widowed, single-parent families, career singles, and retirees.

Once a need is discovered, a ministry must be provided. Remember that love makes a way. It is not enough to identify the need; we must identify with the needy. This may require us to rethink our concepts of ministry for special situations.

In beginning a new ministry, consult with others who have such ministries. Their experience can be valuable. Also, the various departments of our national headquarters can provide excellent resources for ministry to special needs. Don't overlook the possibility that some of these groups, especially if they are separated by cultural barriers, may need a church of their own. Maybe God wants your church to help them.

Create New Units of Ministry

Be certain the Sunday school is grouped properly according to age, even if it means small classes. Develop adult electives to meet the needs of special groups within the church. Organize home Bible study groups and fellowship cells. Be certain that they fit into the great goals of the church and do not become ends in themselves.

New units grow fastest. Starting new units of ministry must be primarily based on two factors, need and available leadership. Be careful that you do not overwork the willing few. Determine priorities of ministry instead of attempting to do everything.

Plan some ministries that do not require people to come into your church building in order to hear the gospel.

Recruit and Train Workers

Growth requires laborers. Jesus' one prayer request was that we would "pray ye therefore the Lord of the harvest, that he will send forth laborers into his harvest" (Matthew 9:38). We can provide better tools (to elaborate on the analogy). A farmer with a tractor will accomplish more than one with horses. Training can be given in how to use the tools. Sometimes people hook the old methods to the new, like a tractor being pulled by horses. Give attention to proper motivation and recognition that will increase effort. Finally, increase the number of workers.

A worker seldom performs in a manner superior to the way he is recruited. A person who is manipulated into teaching a class after he has arrived at church on Sunday morning will determine that the position is not very important. If the superintendent didn't think it necessary to recruit someone until Sunday morning then it surely is okay to study the lesson late Saturday night.

Leadership must be constantly planning ahead. We should now be recruiting people to be trained so that adequate staff will be ready for future ministries.

An excellent approach to training is the *Fundamentals for Sunday School Workers* series (available from Gospel Publishing House). These four units of study emphasize the Sunday school's ministry, Bible study, specific doctrines, and teaching methods. An elective class for training teachers during the Sunday school hour is ideal. Use your best teacher to instruct the class. This way he can multiply his skills by the lives of others.

Another avenue of training is recruiting people to assist experienced teachers as classroom workers where they learn by observation and involvement. The apprentice plan has many benefits. It is easier to recruit people to share responsibility. Follow-up and planning can be shared. Teaching time is increased because the lead teacher does not have to take roll, count the offering, etc. Discipline is much improved. A better worker/pupil ratio results, and better relationships will mean more learning.

Good recruiting takes place on a personal basis. Certain general things should be done. First, survey the interests, skills, and experience of the people. Second, give visibility to the ministries of the workers. Make it exciting to be involved. Finally, assist your workers in improving their self-image by investing time and money in helping them succeed. When workers are happy, fulfilled, and enthusiastic, others will want to become part of the team. Remember how Tom Sawyer got the fence painted?

Provide Additional Space

Growing churches are constantly facing needs for space. They usually have building plans on the drawing board and are raising funds for expansion. But you can do some things while waiting on the contractor.

Be certain you are using space to the optimum. Be sure that classes are fitted to the rooms. Avoid allowing any particular department to feel that a certain classroom is their domain.

Creatively schedule your Sunday school and worship. Why not use the auditorium during the Sunday school hour for children's church? Consider letting the youth and adults use the elementary classrooms during the first hour and the children during the worship hour.

A popular dual-schedule used by several growing churches is simultaneous Sunday school and worship services. These are arranged like this:

Hour 1	Adult electives	Worship service
	Elementary classes	
	Preschool hour 1	
Hour 2	Adult electives	Worship service
	Children's church	
	Youth classes	
	Preschool hour 2	

Some have even gone to two different Sunday schools, each with a different staff, and two different worship services. These are arranged like this:

Hour 1	Sunday school A
Hour 2	Worship service A
Hour 3	Sunday school B
Hour 4	Worship service B

Duel-scheduling has its pros and cons, however. Nevertheless, many who were forced into dual-scheduling because of overcrowding now say they would continue optional schedules even if they could afford adequate space. In our modern society, people like the choices of time.

Don't overlook both teaching and outreach ministries at other times on Sunday and other days of the week.

When building, be sure that all rooms can have multiple uses. In today's economy we must make maximum use of our buildings.

Train Soul Winners, Altar Workers, and Follow-Up Staff

We need both Andrews and Barnabases. Andrew brought people to Jesus. Barnabas helped them become a part of the fellowship.

Most churches challenge people to win others to Christ, but fail to show them how. Both Lifestyle Evangelism, developed by the Assemblies of God Men's Ministries, and Evangelism Explosion III International, headed by D. James Kennedy, are being effectively used to help persons with an interest in personal witnessing develop their gifts.

Altar workers must be able to explain how to accept Christ as Saviour. There should also be trained individuals who specialize in follow-up for each new convert.

Teach your people the priority of friendliness. Use greeters at the door who know the faces of the regular attenders and can quickly identify and help a first-time visitor find his way to the appropriate classroom.

Encourage people to be "given to hospitality." An invitation to a visiting family to share Sunday dinner can be very effective.

Increase Visibility

A choice location, beautiful buildings, radio/TV ministry, or burgeoning attendance all increase the community's awareness of a church. But what if you don't have, or can't afford these things?

The church's visibility can be increased in many inexpensive ways. One small church in Illinois has a good neighbor day, when the youth go out into the community and help people in any way they desire. This is not done for money but simply to express good will to the community.

Another pastor made certain that every service station operator on main street could direct people to the church. Ministries to shut-ins and nursing homes create a positive image in the community's eyes.

Certainly you will want to consider advertising and media ministry. Identify with TV and radio ministries, such as *Revivaltime* and *Every Day With Jesus,* which are beamed into your community. The Office of Information, 1445 Boonville, Springfield, MO 65802, can supply you with many helps for billboards, radio/TV spots, preparing news releases, and evangelism.

Develop a logo. A logo is a sort of trademark. In smaller communities that A/G shield will be adequate. In larger communities you may want to create a unique logo of your own. Use it on your stationery, in all advertising, and prominently on your church sign.

Be certain that signs directing people to your church are placed on major roadways. These signs are available from Gospel Publishing House.

Set Goals and Establish Priorities

Set numerical goals in the growth of enrollment, attendance, budget, workers, and units of ministry. Set long-range and intermediate goals.

Plan ahead. Determine what you feel is a reasonable growth rate and project your attendance for each of the next five years. Determine your needs for space, workers, classes, finances, and new ministries at each stage of growth. Remember that attendance growth and ministry goals interact. You will not grow unless you reach your goals in these other important areas.

Maintain Balance of Outreach and Nurture Ministries

"Enlarge the place of thy tent, and let them stretch forth the curtains of thine habitations: spare not, lengthen thy cords, and strengthen thy stakes" (Isaiah 54:2). Remember every time you lengthen the cords of outreach you must strengthen the stakes of ministry, finances, and the spiritual life of your own church families.

6

Children and Sunday School Growth

Mary rushed home after class one Sunday morning. With the excitement that only children can show, she burst through the door saying, "Papa, Papa! Will you be my guest at Sunday School next week? You see, Papa, if I bring a guest, I'll get a star after my name. You will go, won't you, Papa?"

All week Mary kept prodding her father, expecting him to make that star appear after her name. When Sunday morning came, she and her father walked hand-in-hand toward the small church. He was humming the tunes he heard coming from the Sunday school, which had already started. They were songs he had learned as a boy. He said, "Mary, I'm just going to the door with you, and no farther." "But Papa," she exclaimed, "I won't get my star!" "Well, I'll wave my hand in the door to the superintendent so he'll know I came, then I'll go home," he said. Just as they reached the door, the superintendent greeted them. "Good morning, Paxson! It's good to see you. Come on in." And in to Sunday school they went.

Stephen Paxson was living in a small Indiana town in the early 1800s with his wife, Sara, and their family when he was introduced to Sunday school by his own little daughter. He became captivated with it. In fact he became a Sunday school missionary whose life was devoted to reaching boys and girls. He moved to the Mississippi valley with his family and launched the Mississippi Valley Enterprise under the auspices of the American Sunday School Union. Riding his horse "Robert Raikes," he traveled throughout the region establishing Sunday schools in every village and crossroads. In seven years he established 1,314 Sunday schools with a total enrollment of over 83,000 boys and girls! Many of those Sunday schools became great churches reaching thousands of families for God. The Bible says, "A little child shall lead them." In Stephen Paxson's case, the little child was his daughter.

This is not an isolated incident. During the 200 years of the Sunday school's existence, millions of people have been brought into the church and won to the kingdom of God because someone was motivated to bring a guest. Often, it was a child who was motivated by a simple little star.

Our goal must always be to reach the entire family. Not until we reach the family will we fulfill the Great Commission as it relates to us and our community. Remember the story in Mark chapter 10 when people brought little children to Jesus, and the disciples rebuked them? There is no doubt that Jesus would have us bring the children to Him, for He said, "Forbid them not." On the other hand we must not focus our attention exclusively on the children and forget the adults. The New Testament makes clear that our Lord's desire was for the entire household to be saved. When Zaccheus slid down the tree, Jesus announced to him, "This day is salvation come to thy house." When Peter recounted his vision to the Apostles and Cornelius, he told them the angel had clearly directed him to share the gospel with all men, both Jew and Gentile, "Whereby thou, and all thy house, shall be saved." How can we do anything less than direct our efforts to the entire family and bring them into the knowledge of our wonderful Lord?

Preparing for Growth Through Children

The Necessity of Prayer

Every plan, every activity, and every program ought to be saturated with prayer. We must have the power of the

Holy Spirit to lead us in accomplishing His will. Prayer will equip us for the task of winning our children for the kingdom of God. We must pray for understanding as we plan an organized approach and strategy. Through prayer, the Holy Spirit will give us the wisdom we need for this task. "If any of you lack wisdom, let him ask of God, that giveth to all men liberally, and upbraideth not; and it shall be given him" (James 1:5).

The Necessity of a Positive Attitude

Each teacher must recognize the importance of his teaching gift to the church and believe that he can fulfill his role in the body of Christ. It isn't necessarily the ability a teacher has, or does not have; it is the way he sees himself in the light of the job to be done. When a teacher knows he is called of God, has a commitment to do the job, and believes that he can do it, he will be successful.

Too many teachers are timid, often under the guise of humility. A teacher cannot perform in a manner inconsistent with the way he sees himself. His self-image must be positive. One way to develop a more positive self-image as a teacher is to expand one's vision. The teacher must be helped to believe that his class can grow; then he must prepare for it. If the teacher is unprepared for the addition of new students, much of the effort that goes into bringing them in will be lost, for it will be difficult to hold them. Teachers must do their very best, whether for two or two hundred. In order to do that, the teacher must feel positive about his gift and his ability to perform as he is empowered by the Holy Spirit.

The Necessity of Goals

All teachers must have clearly defined goals toward which they are working. Failure to set goals for growth is to set a goal for no growth. Enrollment, attendance, visitation, and program goals are an important part of the teacher's responsibility. Once the goals are set, we can begin to ask, "How will we reach our goals?" The answer to this question will lead us to procedures designed to reach children.

The Necessity of a Trained Staff

Make plans to recruit and train new workers. One of the most frequently heard complaints from pastors and superintendents is, "We can't get workers," or, "We can't get our people to do anything." With this attitude, they are right! Negative attitudes can be contagious, but the opposite is also true. If you will believe that God can provide people who will dedicate themselves to the task, and if you will ask the Holy Spirit to help you find these people, then you can begin to find the solution to this problem. If potential teachers know they will be trained, they will feel more positive about accepting the job. You can raise your attendance to a record level through promotion, but you will be unable to retain them if you do not have trained workers. Trained workers form a positive basis for growth. Consider using the *Fundamentals for Sunday School Workers* series as the initial training program.

The Necessity of New Classes

Beginning new classes is a tried and tested way to grow that most churches can use. However, many Sunday schools have limited facilities that are already filled. If your building has classes in every corner, find another building where you can organize some new classes. A house next door or across the street can provide additional space. An educational addition to your building may even be in order. When you really want it, you can always find some space somewhere nearby for another Sunday school class. It is best to move the older children or youth to nearby buildings, making room in the church for additional children's classes. Consider a toddler's class. If your beginner class is large, provide a class for the four-year-olds and another for the five-year-olds.

Have you provided a middler class for the elementary children? What about dividing the primary class into a first and second grade division? There are lots of possibilities! Remember, you will never have another class until you start it!

The Necessity of Equipment

Do you have enough chairs? Is there enough curriculum material? Do you use tables for the children to sit around? A table can be a detriment to growth. Only so many chairs can fit around a table, and when the chairs are full, it conveys a message to the teacher that the class is full. Consequently, he no longer works toward growth. It also conveys a negative message to the pupils such as, "You're late. You will have to sit outside the circle because we do not have room for you." When this occurs you have three options: (1) continue as you are but do not expect growth, (2) remove the table to provide room for more pupils, or (3) add another table if the room is large enough for it. If you remove the table, you can provide lap boards for writing and/or handwork.

The Necessity of a Warm Welcome

New children who come into your Sunday school may forget what the lesson was about, the songs you sang and the memory verse, but they will never forget whether you have been friendly. Friendliness is a crucial ingredient the Sunday school can cultivate to hold the newcomer, and it must be planned. Never depend on it to just happen! If possible, have a reception desk in the foyer to welcome all visitors. The receptionist should show a warm and friendly attitude. Ask the child's name. Record it, along with other information, on a first-timer card. The receptionist should have a good knowledge of the Sunday school classroom layout and the names of the teachers, so that she can direct the visitors to the proper class. The teacher should warmly welcome the new pupil and introduce him to the other students in the class. The visitor should feel wanted and appreciated.

Now that we have given attention to these details, let us proceed to consider programs for growth.

The Nursery

The nursery is not an area designed for baby-sitting. It is a child's first experience in church. Babies don't come to Sunday school alone. Someone has to bring them, and it is usually the parents. This provides a unique opportunity for evangelism and growth. If we can develop a plan for building attendance in the nursery, more adults in Sunday school are certain.

Babies can be taught in the nursery! What splendid opportunities are present from week to week to teach children about loving, caring, and sharing with simple Bible stories and songs. A small child can respond to all types of impressions created by the teacher as she uses each lesson to carefully build character and lay foundations for life.

If your nursery ministers only to those babies born to church families, however, its growth will be slow. Look around your community. Scores of families with infants and small children never attend Sunday school, and they can be reached by providing ministry to the baby. Remember the adage that suggests, "The whole world loves a baby!"

For simplicity, group all children from birth to two as babies you desire to reach. Next, design a campaign to reach them that will contribute to the growth of the Sunday school. An example is discussed below.

Baby Day

Organize a "baby alert." Use a group of ladies from the neighborhood and other friendship circles. They will know who has had or is expecting a baby. Two to three months before the Sunday that has been designated Baby Day, gather information from the families with new babies.

Include family names, addresses, and babies' names and birth dates.

Have the pastor send a letter of congratulations to the parents, inviting them to participate in Baby Day. Participation will involve attendance, a gift and photos for the baby, dedication of the child, and the promise of a beautiful and valuable dedication certificate. Include in the letter a return card or envelope so the parents may accept the invitation.

Allow two or three weeks for the parents to respond. For those who do not, assign a follow-up team to visit the home and extend a personal invitation. To those who respond send a letter containing specific instructions, including the date, time, place, etc. The unchurched people should be given special attention during this process. Most unchurched people do not understand our procedure of dedicating infants. However, it is almost universally accepted that something of a religious nature should be done for the new baby. Follow-up teams will need to explain what is done and why. You will find it surprising how unchurched people will respond to your invitation. The pastor should conduct a preliminary class for the parents to explain the purpose of dedication and to share the gospel. Remember that most adults are converted during a time of stress, and a new baby in the home is such a time.

Decorate for the occasion. Have people bring large stuffed animals to place around the church. Pink and blue colors are always acceptable. Plan for special music using a "cherub" choir. A small gift for each child would be appropriate. Ask a camera buff from your congregation to serve as photographer for the day.

Ask the parents to bring their babies to the altar where the pastor can perform the dedication. Customarily, the pastor's wife assists in the ceremony. The dedication certificate should be presented to the parents at this time. Have sufficient nursery workers on hand to take all the babies into the nursery immediately following dedication.

This will enable the parents to give their full attention to the service. The pastor should offer a sermon appropriate to this unique occasion.

At the conclusion of the service, photograph each baby. Offer the photo to the parents when they return next week, or plan a special showing of baby pictures the following Sunday evening. In a church that uses this program annually, a sizeable library of baby pictures will be built. When the church announces the showing of baby pictures, it will attract widespread attention! In just a few years, growing children will be able to see their own dedication pictures.

Baby Day is not limited to the Sunday school hour, nor is the Sunday school hour excluded. Upon arrival, parents should be instructed to take their baby directly to the nursery so they and the baby can enjoy Sunday school. The church might consider providing enough workers to return the babies to their parents at the close of the hour. The morning service would proceed as described above.

A simple program like this does not require a lot of special talent, and it costs very little. Any church, large or small, can use Baby Day for growth and evangelism. The possibilities for reaching young adult parents are tremendous!

We're Expecting

Baby Day is an example of what a Sunday school can do to reach out to young families. Consider now a campaign lasting four to six weeks, designed to build attendance in the nursery class. "We're Expecting" is a theme with which mothers can identify. Name the Sunday themes of the campaign: (1) "We're Expecting Faithfulness," (2) "We're Expecting Love," (3) "We're Expecting Growth," (4) "We're Expecting Fun." Each week focus the emphasis around the given theme.

Design a small book for each baby with his/her name on the cover. Each Sunday record the weight, clothing, items of special interest, etc., on a card and place it in the baby's book.

At the end of the campaign, the book can be presented to the mother as a keepsake. Each Sunday the baby is present, put a small gift with a note in his diaper bag. The note can be a personal message from the teacher to the parents, reflecting on the baby's traits.

Beginners

Beginners are growing rapidly and their physical environment is constantly expanding. The development of their intellectual abilities creates an intense hunger for learning. Opportunities for spiritual development abound. An important link in that development is building bridges of friendship. So, it is important that we help beginners establish social relationships. Every child who comes to Sunday school has friends in the neighborhood where he lives. It is easy for most children this age to make friends. If he has had a pleasant experience in Sunday school, the child naturally would want to invite his friends to come with him.

Knowing this, it is possible to develop a community outreach with beginners as the missionaries. A wide variety of themes can attract their attention and involvement. Some themes to consider are school, army, the circus, and traffic. Using the army theme, for example, pupils are enlisted to become soldiers for the Lord. Each class becomes a platoon or company. A recruitment center is set up to register all new pupils. Each boy or girl who brings a friend receives a promotion in rank. If possible, have a man and/or woman dressed in service uniform to talk to the boys and girls one Sunday. Decorate the classroom to support the theme.

Every child loves the circus, because it means animals and clowns. Decorate the classroom like the big top. Crepe paper streamers can be strung from the center of the room to the walls, giving the impression of a tent. Fix small fuzzy animals with a pin to a large bulletin board. This will attract lots of attention! Each child who brings a new pupil receives one of the fuzzy animals as an award. Use puppets. Dress someone, perhaps the storyteller, as a clown. He will not only draw attention with his funny antics, but will tell a character-building story, and urge every child to bring a friend next Sunday. With special emphasis like this once or twice each year, beginners can be enlisted as a very positive influence in the growth of the Sunday school.

Primaries, Middlers, and Juniors

Boys and girls in the elementary grades are very competitive, and can be easily challenged to participate in exciting promotions that will bring growth to the Sunday school. These children have a high energy level and will jump at an opportunity to perform in some manner that promises rewards. Special efforts to reach new children should be scheduled at least twice each year in the spring and fall. Here is an example of a spring campaign.

Most smaller churches support the district summer camping program, and some larger churches sponsor their own camps for children. Why not have a Go-to-Camp campaign for these elementary children? Offer scholarships to boys and girls when they attain a certain number of points. Score them each Sunday for attendance, bringing visitors, having their Bibles, learning the memory verse, etc. The necessary funds for the scholarships can be obtained through special offerings and individual donors. An appeal to the congregation to "send a child to camp" prompts people to contribute paying a camper's way.

As a further incentive to the children, purchase two inexpensive suitcases, one for the boys and one for the girls. Each Sunday add some camping item to the suitcase; a flashlight, a Bible, a T-shirt, $2.00 spending money, etc. At the close of the campaign, award the suitcases to the ones who brought the most pupils.

Additional Outreach Ministries

A wide range of ministries and programs have been developed by the Assemblies of God. These are used successfully to reach children, win them to the Lord, and promote growth in the Sunday school.

Vacation Bible School

Vacation Bible School is one of the most fruitful ways to reach and win children for the Lord during the summer months. Though VBS provides an excellent opportunity for teaching, more important, it provides a strong evangelistic endeavor. Many churches have expanded the VBS to include the entire family, classes being held during the evening hours. A big advantage of VBS is its requirement of many people. Lasting growth demands local lay involvement. When promoted properly, VBS can be one of the most productive efforts of a church.

Kids Crusades

This program is widely used by many churches. It is not as seasonal as VBS. Usually a child evangelist is called to employ his special skills in the ministry of reaching children. This program is remarkably successful! What child can resist singing, clowns, stories, puppets, prizes, games, etc.? Some churches are fortunate to have skilled personnel on the staff who conduct their own crusades.

Royal Rangers

This is a program for boys between the ages of 5 and 17 years. Because of its similarity to scouting, it has a wide appeal, attracting churched and nonchurched boys. They are divided into five age groups: Straight Arrows, ages 5-6; Buckaroos, ages 7-8; Pioneers, ages 9-11; Trailblazers, ages 12-14; Trail-Sea-Air Rangers, ages 15-17. It is an effective means of reaching boys, providing a wholesome outlet for their natural inclination to enjoy the outdoors.

Missionettes

Similar to Royal Rangers, Missionettes is the girls' version of scouting. Designed for those between ages 5 and 15 years, it is also an effective outreach for girls in and outside the church. It is divided into four age groups: Daisies, ages 5-6; Prims, ages 7-8; Juniors, ages 9-11; and Seniors, ages 12-15.

Children's Church

Many churches, of all sizes, have developed effective worship services for children, which are usually conducted in a separate auditorium while the regular Sunday adult service takes place. This special service is planned for children and presents a meaningful worship and learning experience at their level.

In larger churches having proper facilities, the children are grouped by grade into several age-level children's churches, such as preschool, grades 1-3, and grades 4-6. Children are seldom kept in children's church past the sixth grade.

Bus Ministry

Providing Sunday school buses to bring people to church has been a very effective ministry. Sunday schools such as Elmira Christian Center, Elmira, New York; Victoria Tabernacle, Kansas City, Kansas; and The People's Church, Arnold, Missouri, have been running buses successfully for many years. Thousands are brought in to be taught and to hear the gospel. The persistent and determined use of this evangelistic tool, by them as well as many others, has resulted in success. Normally, the number of children riding the buses far outnumber the adults. However, with a planned follow-up, the child who rides the bus can open the door of his home to the entire family.

Excellent helps for all these outreach ministries are available from the Gospel Publishing House, 1445 Boonville, Springfield, MO 65802.

7

Youth, Adults, and Sunday School Growth

Sunday school is not just for kids. It is for all ages. Youth and adults who suggest that Sunday school is too juvenile have not really understood what it is about. Everyone needs to be taught the Word of God at his appropriate age level. The Bible is a book for all ages, and we should have classes for all ages. Building exciting youth and adult classes is crucial to Sunday school growth and is one of the great needs of today's church.

Youth

The moment a child is born and the umbilical cord is cut, he begins a separation from his parents. The nursery child spends almost all his time with parents. The beginner child spends 10 percent of his time away from his parents, the primary child, 20 percent. When he becomes a junior child, his time away increases to 40 percent. By the time he is a teenager, he may spend as much as 90 percent of his time away from his parents. The church, and particularly the Sunday school, must help fill the vast amount of time a teen spends away from home and family. I believe that all youth programs and activities in the church should be coordinated. The Sunday school youth program and the broader church youth program must be working together, complementing and supporting each other.

Larger churches that can afford a youth pastor should have him supervise the youth department in the Sunday school and, perhaps, teach one of the classes. Smaller churches that have only two youth classes should appoint those teachers to the youth council. This will add strength.

If your Sunday school is going to reach out to youth, it must be relevant and consider characteristic needs of today's young people. We cannot have Sunday school as we did 30 years ago. Then, there were few TV's, no shopping centers, no programmed recreation in urban areas, no fast-food restaurants, no jet airlines, no air conditioning, no computers, no satellite communications, no medicare, and 1,000 other things! To utilize an approach to Sunday school using the same arrangement of classes, a stereotyped method of teaching, and the same words and phrases from 30 years ago will discourage the teenager. We are living in a different world today. If we are going to communicate with today's teens, we must be willing to break with the traditions of the past and speak in the language they understand. We must not be afraid to innovate and be creative.

Consider your Sunday school records. If you have a good enrollment among primaries, middlers, and juniors, but see it begin to drop among junior highs, and drop even further among senior highs, you have a problem. You are losing people! It is a sad statistic that more pupils are lost from the Sunday school at age 16 than at any other age. The average boy or girl enters Sunday school at age 5 and leaves at age 15. The breakdown for dropouts is as follows:

26% leave between ages 11-14

50% leave between ages 15-17

24% leave at age 18 and up

Those who teach the teen classes in your Sunday school should be some of the very best teachers available. We must understand that we are losing too many teens at the most opportune time to evangelize them.

Lionel A. Hunt gives these statistics of conversions in America:

1% were converted under age 4
85% were converted between ages 4 and 15
10% were converted between ages 15 and 30
4% were converted when older than 30 years
of age

George W. Truett, famous Baptist pastor, took a survey of 1,200 men and found that

3 were converted when over 45 years old
13 were converted between ages 40 and 45
Less than 30 were converted when over 30
1,100 were converted when under 21

These surveys should emphasize how important it is to train good youth teachers, organize attractive youth classes, develop active programs, and build a strong outreach to teens. Young people have a keen interest in spiritual things.

Furthermore, our concern must extend beyond the young people in our church; we must also be concerned about the many youth who are unreached. They have an awakening curiosity about religion. That is seen in the fact that so many are caught up in cults and Eastern religions. Youth are serious in their quest for faith. They have a desire to believe in something or someone. They are searching for meaning and fulfillment and they want release from guilt. We have a wonderful Saviour to share with them. When the gospel is presented to them properly, many accept Him. It is significant that many of the great revivals throughout church history have begun among young people. We must have the courage to revamp our educational programs to reach out to the youth of our community, or we will miss one of the greatest opportunities of our day.

Developing Strong Teen Classes

If you want to see growth in your youth department, you must have a good understanding of today's teens, what their needs are, and how to structure a program that will meet those needs.

Understanding Them

1. Teens are searching for knowledge. Since they are young, they lack experience. While they are beginning to accumulate experience, they have acquired a great amount of knowledge. There is so much secular knowledge they receive. The teen Sunday school class is the best device we have to impart Biblical knowledge.

2. Teens are idealistic. When they see hypocrisy, deceit, and double standards, they become cynical and mistrusting. The teen teacher must be a model of trust and faith. His personal example to the class is far more important than what he has to say.

3. Teens are impressionable. Many good and bad habits are developed in the teen years, and they last for life! The tobacco companies know this, and that is why their advertising is almost totally slanted to the young in heart. It is significant that the vast majority of missionaries felt called to the mission field while in their teens. When missionaries visit your church they should always be requested to spend some time with the youth.

4. Teens are zealous. They are quick to rally around a cause. Offer your teens the cause of Christ, and enlist them to witness for Him and bring their friends into the Kingdom. Teenagers can really get excited about Christ. They willingly give themselves, often with sacrifice, to follow His cause.

5. Teens are visionary. They have dreams and plans for the future. The Bible says, "Your young men shall see visions" (Acts 2:17). The wise Sunday school teacher will help them plan a course in life where their visions and dreams can find direction and fulfillment.

Know Their Needs

Some teen teachers try to build fences around their students, then spend most of their teaching time trying to keep them inside the fences. Those who work with youth must give them a chance to grow up! They do not become adults overnight!

1. Teens need acceptance. Because they are so self-conscious at this time in life, they may wonder if the changes they are going through have altered their position with the teacher. He must reassure them and communicate his love, accepting them as they are.

2. Teens need love. Every person reaches out for love and acceptance. A teen will do almost anything to be accepted and loved—at least by his peers. You will have to find ways of saying, "I love you," over and over again. Use every opportunity to express love: face-to-face meetings, the phone, cards and letters, casual meetings, and so much more. Be sure to remember their birthdays with a card that expresses acceptance, love, and personal concern.

3. Teens need self-esteem. A great tragedy among our young people today is the epidemic of inferiority. They have feelings of inadequacy and incompetence, and have a difficult time accepting themselves. This finds expression in the drug culture, rebellion, discontent, and hostility. Teens need to know they have been created by God for a divine purpose. When they realize they have value and that there is a divine plan for everyone, then their lives will have meaning.

4. Teens need guidance. The church has great responsibilities and opportunities to guide youth through the difficult years of adolescence. Sunday school teachers can be a significant influence in the lives of searching teens.

5. Teens need activity. Remember what was said earlier. Ninety percent of teen time is spent away from their parents. For that reason the church should provide a variety of activities for these energetic young people. These activities can include Sunday school, youth meetings, witnessing,

camps, retreats, social events, and more. There can never be too many, and they must all be appealing.

6. Teens need friends. The Sunday school provides one of the best opportunities anywhere for young people to make friends. Introduce every new teen by name. Help him to get acquainted with others in the class. Make sure he begins to make some new friends the very first time he attends. One of the keys to keeping a visitor is to make sure he finds friends.

7. Teens need Jesus. The teen teacher should be a skilled soul winner who takes time to deal with each teen personally. Winning them to the Lord cannot be left to chance. The teacher must go out of his way to provide each teen with an opportunity to be saved. A visit to his home, a visit to your home, an evening out, lunch or dinner, after class talks, and many other opportunities can be arranged.

Provide Outreach Activities

A Sunday school that aggressively reaches out to young people will have a full social events calendar for them: parties, banquets, hikes, hayrides, field trips, sports, etc. Each of these should be well planned, with special invitations for each teen to bring an unchurched friend.

In addition to social events, the teen Sunday school classes should develop challenging campaigns that will motivate the members to bring their friends to Sunday school. Here are a few ideas:

Civil War. Main Street in town becomes the Mason-Dixon line. All who live on one side will be the North and those on the other side, the South. Give identification pins or ribbons to everyone. Confederate money, printed on the church copier, can be given for each friend brought. This will be exchanged for admission tickets to a special event or concert at the conclusion of the campaign.

Travel Theme. This can be used in conjunction with the annual missionary convention. Highlight a different country each Sunday. Teachers can dress in the costumes of that country. Have the missionary speak and show some items from the country in which he is serving. At the conclusion have an international feast.

Political Theme. The fall is a good time to emphasize this theme. Divide the class into two parties. Hang banners and posters. Have a ballot box. Give notes to those who bring a friend. Campaign speeches each Sunday would be in order. (Candidates tell why teens should be Christians.) Conclude with a victory rally and lots of food!

Adults

The church and Sunday school must give special consideration to adults. The strength of the church in all ages has been its ability to reach and win adults. It is relatively easy to win the children. They have few established convictions, deeply ingrained traditions, or hang-ups to overcome. They respond quickly and easily, and are saved without convincing debate or earnest persuasion. The bus ministry, child evangelism, and other efforts have all proved their effectiveness in reaching children. But, what about adults? What efforts are being made to reach the moms and dads? We must not allow our Sunday schools to focus entirely on children. We must accept the challenge of reaching adults.

The church should not lose sight of the fact that 90 percent of all workers are adult and 80 percent of all financial giving comes from adults. If we can reach and win more adults we will have the workers we need to fulfill the purpose of God in our community, and we will have the finances to pay the bills.

Survey of Unchurched Americans

The Princeton Religion Research Center and the Gallup organization (American Institute of Public Opinion) conducted a survey of unchurched Americans in 1952, 1965, and 1978. For the purpose of charting these people, an unchurched person was defined as one who was not a member of a church or synagogue in the last six months, apart from weddings, funerals, or special holidays. The survey disclosed 61 million American adults who were unchurched. Many of them, although not drawn to organized religion, had positive inclinations toward religion and felt that "religion is a good thing." In fact, the overwhelming majority of the unchurched said they would like to have their children receive religious training.

Slightly more than half of the unchurched (52 percent or about 32 million adults) said they could envision a situation in which they could become a "fairly active member of a church now." They also said they would be open to an invitation from the church community. Studying the Gallup survey helps us discover four conditions unchurched adults want from the church they would attend. They describe these conditions of the church in the following way:

1. It must be a church that would listen to their religious doubts and spiritual needs.

2. It must be a church with vital worship and preaching.

3. It must be a church with a real thirst for Christian education at its best.

4. It must be a church that will simply invite them to join. (What a challenge this should be to us!)

If this survey is accurate, we must realize that every church in America is surrounded by a large number of unchurched adults who really do want to attend. We must proceed at once to develop programs in the church that will meet the needs of unchurched people.

Find the Needs of Your Adults

Every community has a different complex of adults. Some retirement communities are specifically for senior adults. Some are bedroom communities with both husband and wife working out of the house. Some areas consist mainly of single adults. Look around your community. Do some research. Visit the library and check the community statistics. You might even visit the local laundromat for half a day and talk with the people who patronize it. Check your local newspaper to see what services are being marketed. Knock on a few doors. Get information from the people living on each block. Once you discover the type of community you have and how many adults are there, you can proceed to structure programs that will attract the attention of these people and draw them in.

Create an Atmosphere

Unfortunately, many adult classes operate as if they were planned in 1890! Like teen classes—adult classes need creativity and innovation. More than anything, adults want Christian education that is relevant and will teach them how to function in a complex, confused world. Be willing to make changes in this direction. If you want to attract adults to your Sunday school, here are some things you should do.

1. *Look at your grouping.* Adults resist being grouped by age or by sex. Some Sunday schools have established young adult classes with age restrictions between 25 and 35. At first, everyone is very happy; but if the class has an aggressive outreach, class members will bring their friends; and then the friends will bring more friends. Unless someone stands at the door to check ages each Sunday, within six months the class will have adults from ages 20 to 60! The only reasonable way to group adults is by interest.

Offer a large auditorium class that has no age or sex restrictions and that is taught by a *skilled* teacher. Let this class become the doorway for most adults coming into the Sunday school. After taking this class they are to be directed to elective classes to meet their particular needs. Develop as many additional classes as your facilities will allow, and secure skilled teachers. Never *assign* adults to classes. Give them the option of choosing the class they want to attend.

Depending on the particular age-level needs, it is usually helpful to organize classes for singles, senior adults, etc.

2. *Check the arrangement of your classes.* Having two or more classes in the same room is very difficult and should be avoided whenever possible. Only one class should occupy a room and it should be protected against interference and disturbances.

Are you in a classroom sitting around tables? This can deter growth among adult groups as it can in children's classes. If you are going to use tables, use a large room and be prepared to add as many tables as may be necessary to match your growth.

Are you in the auditorium? Are all the members gathered on one side, clustered in the rear, or scattered throughout the area? Look at your arrangement through the eyes of a visitor. What does he think when he comes a bit late and sees all the adults in the three back pews. How does he feel when there is no way for him to enter without embarrassment? If the members are scattered, do they give the impression they are not getting along? Where does the teacher stand? Is he between the pews or halfway down the aisle? Does this convey to the visitor an admission of catering to the people because they refuse to move forward? Your room arrangement can convey a variety of psychological messages! It is best for the teacher to stand front and center, with the members toward the front, exhibiting an atmosphere of interest and expectancy. Arrange your class so that it says positive things about your class.

3. *Plan the curriculum.* The standard adult curriculum is a seven-year continuous study through the entire Bible. It emphasizes the most important Biblical passages and truths. Excellent helps are provided for the teacher in the quarterly "PATH" packet. Many adult classes follow this series.

When your research reveals special groups of adults with special needs, you may want to project a series of lessons outside the regular seven-year cycle. Provision for this is made in the wide selection of Radiant Life electives. Here you will find topic studies, family life studies, verse-by-verse Bible studies, prophetic studies, and many others. All you need do is match the curriculum to your needs and you can have a most interesting class.

Seven for Heaven

Here is a program planned and used by David Watson, pastor of Bethel Assembly of God, Girard, Pennsylvania. Pastor Watson's church joined the district Sunday School Crusade and, using this program for eight consecutive years, won the first place award six times, and second place twice. Each year the church experienced a 20 percent growth and held it. During that period attendance went from 65 to 245, and most of the growth was among adults. They also completed a building program to accommodate their growing numbers. Here is the program:

The Plan. Twelve couples are selected from the congregation as team captains. New converts make the best team captains because they have a wider contact with the unsaved community. Once the team captains are chosen, the Sunday school enrollment, junior high and up, is divided equally among the twelve teams. (Small Sunday schools may choose to have fewer teams, and large Sunday schools may have to double the number.)

The team captain is responsible for contacting each member of his team weekly to insure their attendance and to see that they bring a friend. Meet with all team captains two weeks prior to the campaign and review all details.

The Procedure. One week prior to launching the campaign the pastor should preach a sermon to inspire faith in God. Pastor Watson entitles his sermon, "Is There Anything Too Hard for the Lord?" In his message Pastor Watson emphasizes the truth that every Christian has an influence on at least seven unsaved people. Following the sermon, there is an invitation in which everyone is urged to respond.

After prayer together each person is given a card and encouraged to list the names of seven unchurched persons who they will trust God to save during the campaign. This is their "Seven For Heaven" list. During the five week campaign each person making this commitment makes a commitment to those seven persons, praying for them daily, contacting them, and doing everything possible to bring them to Sunday school. Once they are in the church they are fully exposed to the convicting power of the Holy Spirit.

With each team member reaching out to his "Seven" there will be many who respond to the invitation for salvation each Sunday. The pastor will be wise to take the lead by making his own "Seven For Heaven" list, and do his best to have one or more persons there each Sunday. Waves of excitement will be created each week as team members compare their lists, marking those who have made a profession of faith in Christ.

The Follow Up. Once a person has made a commitment, he should receive a new converts packet*, designed to acquaint him with the church and its ministries. He should also be enrolled in a new converts class*. New converts are also enlisted in a support program called the church's Adoption Program*. (*Details for their implementation are given at the end of this chapter.)

The Mechanics. Each team is assigned a goal, which increases every Sunday during the campaign. When the team reaches or exceeds the goal, it receives bonus points. Scoring is simple: each team member present and each visitor brought scores one point. Team members' children are not counted, but visitors' children are.

Keeping the Records. (1) Each team member writes the name(s) of his visitor on a slip of paper and gives it to the team captain before Sunday school begins. (2) The team captain will prepare a master list of all those present counting for his team. (3) The master lists are collected halfway through Sunday school. (4) A Team Progress Board (note explanation at the end of this chapter) is prepared and the progress of all teams is acknowledged just before morning worship begins.

The Awards. At the end of the campaign a banquet will be held for all the teams. The first six teams with the highest scores will be honored. The first place team captains will receive a personal gift or $25.00. Second place team captains will receive a $15.00 gift. Third place team captains will receive a $10.00 gift.

One can easily understand that this campaign is really an encouragement for members to bring their unchurched neighbors and friends to hear the gospel. What rejoicing occurs each Sunday with souls being saved! This is revival!

New Convert Packet

Purpose

The New Convert Packet is made up by the pastor with a number of helps available in the Now That I'm A Christian series of Evangelism Literature for America from the Gospel Publishing House.

Procedure

Following the morning service the new converts are given the New Convert Packet and it is explained. Complete names and addresses and phone numbers are taken for follow-up. The new convert is invited to share in the New Convert Class, which meets on Wednesday evenings at 7 p.m.

New Convert Class

Purpose

This ministry in the church is set up especially for the new convert. It is a class that helps him to understand more about his new found faith in God and helps him to understand the Bible.

Procedure

The class should meet at a time convenient for the local church. It is designed especially for the new convert, allowing him an opportunity to discuss the church, its ministries and doctrine. The class is set up for a 14-week period. The new convert is given a certificate for completing this course.

Adoption Program

Purpose

This ministry in the church is to help the new convert grow in God, experience the love of God, and to feel loved by our church and the people in our church. In helping this child of God grow, allow nothing to take the place of personal contact.

> Beloved, let us love one another: for love is of God; and every one that loveth is born of God, and knoweth God (1 John 4:7).

Procedure

1. Pastor gives an adoption card (with new convert's name, address, and phone number) to an adoption family.

2. The adoption family is to visit the adopted new convert *once a week* for a period of 6 weeks. The pastor will call the adoption family on Friday to get information for the files on the new convert.

3. The adoption family should feel led of the Holy Spirit.

4. The goal during this period is to enable the new convert to feel our church's love and to grow in God.

5. The adoption family is free to take the new convert out to dinner, or to have him visit in their home, or to do an activity with them, cultivating God's love in him.

Team Progress Chart

Purpose

This record will show progress of all the teams for each week of the Crusade. It sparks enthusiasm.

Procedure

Using a 4 x 8 sheet of plywood, place all the team captains' names on the board, allowing space to the right for the week's points and also for the cumulative score of each team. See diagram below.

SEVEN FOR HEAVEN

Team Captains	This Week	Running Total
John and Pat Puline	40	100
Wes and Deb Pettis	50	90
Mike and Joy Gorelikow	80	130
Bob and Dolores McDonald	80	165

8

Growth Campaigns and Promotions

Central Assembly of God had averaged 175 in Sunday school attendance for some time when a visiting friend challenged them. "Why not go for broke!" he said. "You have a great membership dedicated to the work of the Sunday school, and with your pastor's excellent leadership you can double your attendance in 30 days! Are you interested?" They were indeed! All they needed was someone to challenge them and give directions.

The pastor was well aware that his attendance had been on a plateau long enough, and this challenge was all he needed to reach out for growth. He was convinced that if he could get a sense of direction, his staff and his people would follow him. "Tell us how," was his enthusiastic response. Plans for a growth campaign that would double his attendance in 30 days were carefully drawn. Every detail was considered, leaving no room for failure. Schedules were set, assignments were made, and the entire congregation mobilized for an outreach never before attempted. Could they do it?

On the Sunday targeted for double attendance they had 540 present! Even more important, more than 30 people responded to the invitation for salvation. This was a very special effort and the congregation proved to themselves that they could do it! The following Sunday attendance was 260; however, that was 85 more than they had been averaging! From that Sunday on, the attendance never fell below 200. Some Sunday schools never reach out for new people in a concentrated effort because they are afraid of how many they may lose after it is over. Growing Sunday schools never look at what they might lose; they focus on what they will gain.

Many times pastors and workers have been inspired to make a special effort for growth, only to have someone on the staff raise a multitude of problems they would have to face if they chose to organize a campaign for growth. People sometimes cite problems that involve finances, facilities, curriculum materials, transportation, scheduling, and a host of others. After discussing only problems, the objections become so overwhelming that the inspiration is lost, and they decide to do nothing.

Here is a principle that should be learned well: *Always make your decisions before trying to solve all the problems attached to it. When you bring the problem-solving process into decisionmaking, your thinking will become clouded and you will force yourself into the wrong decision.* The battle is won or lost at this point of making decisions to reach out and grow. You must not react negatively to possible problems. They will come. But you can handle them: one at a time, as they arise. Make your decision first, and stick with it. It is the surest way to victory.

Why Have Growth Campaigns?

God wants your Sunday school to grow! How can any church, large or small, rationalize away the responsibilities of the Great Commission? You can recognize the process in such excuses as "Our classrooms are already full so there is no room to bring in more people." "We just love our small church and want to keep it like it is." "We have all the programs we need and do not want to burden our people with outreach." What a travesty! We can never relax our efforts to reach the lost as long as one unsaved person lives in the community.

Take a good look at your Sunday school. What you see is probably the result of what you have made it! Growth is not a will-o'-the-wisp that comes to some and not to others. It is not the product of luck, chance or fate. Rather, growth is the result of well-designed programs, strategies, policies, and procedures. God's will comes into focus when you seek His guidance and leadership. And when you do, the will of God will most certainly lead you into your community to reach the lost.

Most successful Sunday school growth is the direct result of structured campaigns to reach out. *Webster's New Collegiate Dictionary* defines *campaign* as "a connected series of operations designed to bring about a particular result." The word *campaign* is from the French, meaning, "open country suited for military maneuvers." I cannot think of a more fitting word to use in mapping our strategy to go into the world and win the lost. Sunday school campaigns, regardless of their duration, are the most logical and successful way to achieve growth and evangelize your community for God.

Growth rarely happens otherwise. Some people take exception to growth campaigns. They have a fear of contests and other promotions, feeling that to inject competition, incentives, and rewards to motivate people is worldly. Sunday schools with this attitude have a program of sameness, little or no enthusiasm, and a general lackluster attitude. These people usually oppose all forms of extrinsic motivation, feeling that everyone should love God enough to be motivated from within. They say, "Every Christian should participate by bringing his friends, because it is the right thing to do!" They rarely bring their friends or anyone else. Where this philosophy exists you will usually find a stagnant Sunday school, unknown in the community, and content with taking care of their little flock.

There are two basic reasons for a Sunday school becoming involved in a structured campaign:

1. To motivate every leader, teacher, and pupil to be actively involved in the local church's outreach to the unchurched of the community.

2. To attract the attention of the community and let people know the church is in business for God.

A. G. Ward said, "If I were only a shoe-shine boy, I would learn how to snap a rag to attract attention." It pays to advertise the Sunday school through well-planned promotions. How can any Sunday school grow if it fails to attract the attention of people in the community?

Try this little test. Have an out-of-town friend stop at a gas station on the edge of town and inquire of the location and time of services for the local Assembly of God. If the attendant doesn't know this information, it is time for your Sunday school to launch an exciting, soul-winning outreach campaign.

Planning the Campaign

No campaign should ever be a spur-of-the-moment effort. If it is attempted without careful planning, promotion, scheduling, and follow-up, it is doomed to failure. Make the decision, think it through, do the planning, and carry through. You will enjoy growth as a result.

Check the Calendar

Just as nature has a growing season, so does Sunday school. It generally falls between Labor Day and Memorial Day, with some weeks omitted in the middle of winter for those regions that experience severe winters. During these months, two high points for Sunday school and church attendance naturally occur: Christmas and Easter. In our culture, people naturally think of spiritual things during Lent and Advent. Wise leadership will take advantage of this and promote an outreach to touch people at these sensitive times. Therefore, every Sunday school should consider two campaigns each year, lasting from three to six weeks. One should be in the fall, one in the spring. The remainder of the Sunday school year can be highlighted with special days as the need arises.

Schedule Every Important Detail

Start early. Give yourself time to attend to details without undue pressure. Most successful efforts will require a minimum of three months for scheduling.

Countdown	Things to do
12 weeks	Set dates and determine goals
10 weeks	Order printing, banners, awards, etc.
8 weeks	Introduce the campaign to the entire staff.
6 weeks	Introduce the campaign to the entire congregation.
4 weeks	Introduce the campaign in every class.
2 weeks	Complete all props, signs, and decorations.
1 week	Go over all details in a workers conference.
Monday before	Check every detail concerning parking, buses, classrooms, equipment, ushers, music, curriculum, and awards. Leave nothing to chance.
Tuesday before	All final mailings should be posted.
Saturday before	See that all workers are functioning in visitation, phone calls, erecting props, and prayer.
Sunday	The big day has come. Launch the campaign with enthusiasm. Believe God for great victories.

Enthusiastic Leadership

The pastor, general superintendent, department super-intendents, teachers, and even the secretaries *must* get excited about the campaign. They must be enthusiastic about reaching the lost, bringing them into the Sunday school, seeing them converted. If the leaders do not get excited, who else will? Their excited, enthusiastic leadership will be inspirational to everyone else.

Decorations

Appeal to both children and adults with appropriate decorations. They help to create the atmosphere and highlight the theme. Use lots of color. Fill entire walls in the classrooms and departments with the theme. Make it big! Allow the children to participate in the decorations by having a poster contest, all entries displayed throughout the church.

Awards

One of the deepest cravings of people is to feel important and appreciated. It has been estimated that ninety percent of the things we do are prompted by a desire to feel important. *Awards* is a very broad term that includes a variety of things, both done and given. Children are especially open to motivation through awards. Teachers must enthusiastically recognize every new pupil, and the one responsible for bringing him. This kind of appreciation before the entire class is a powerful force in motivating others to bring their friends. Small gifts can be given. A star, a small stuffed animal, a picture, an inexpensive Bible, a candy bar, etc., are all received as an expression of your appreciation for what has been done. Cards, notes, and letters to both children and adult pupils, thanking them and expressing love and appreciation, are all in order.

Assemblies

Most Sunday schools have discontinued the opening

assembly. The pupils go directly to the classroom where the entire Sunday school session is conducted. Although we will not discuss the advantages and disadvantages of this arrangement here, let's give consideration to the assembly as it relates to growth campaigns. Whether or not you have the usual opening and/or closing assembly each Sunday, do have one each Sunday during the campaign.

The purpose for this opening assembly is to promote the campaign and build enthusiasm. Remember the high school pep rallies before the Friday evening football game? The assembly is not called for worship, or for teaching in particular; it is for promotion. An excited department superintendent will talk about the assembly with enthusiasm, encouraging everyone to participate. The theme will be emphasized, the awards displayed, and the rules carefully explained so that everyone will understand procedures. Schedule and plan this assembly for each Sunday of the campaign. It will arouse interest, hold attention, and help sustain momentum. The success of your campaign will largely depend on how well you promote each week. Even the best ideas can be unproductive if they are not supported with good promotion.

Evangelism

In all of the excitement and color we give to promoting a campaign, let us always maintain a right sense of priorities. No one is on an ego trip. We are not working just to have a large number in attendance. The real purpose behind all our planning, scheduling, decorating, promotion, prayer, and hard work is to lead people to Christ. All those involved in the campaign must keep this purpose clearly in focus. Soul winning every Sunday, especially during the campaign, is the real key to success.

Every teacher must be trained in evangelism. Each Sunday the teacher must find time during the class session to present the gospel, urging boys and girls, men and women, to accept Christ as Lord of their lives. With a good campaign, you will have new pupils every Sunday. An alert teacher will employ a variety of methods in presenting the gospel, as well as making an appeal to accept Christ.

When giving an invitation, five things should be kept in mind by the teacher:

1. *Be brief.* After telling the Bible story or presenting the gospel, you do not have to keep repeating what has already been said. There is no need to impress the pupils with the story that has already been told, or the lesson that has been presented. Depend on the Holy Spirit to provide conviction and create a response. Be sensitive to the Holy Spirit.

2. *Be personal.* Use the personal pronoun *you*. When the teacher says, "Does anyone want to accept Christ," he is speaking to no one. It is better to be personal by saying, "Do *you* want to accept Christ?" "Do *you* want to pray?" The pupil will feel you are speaking to him personally.

3. *Be clear.* Whatever appeal you make, it must be clearly understood. Children in particular tend to take everything literally. If you say, "Let Jesus come into your heart," you must explain what you mean by "heart."

4. *Be voluntary.* Do not pressure the pupil into responding. Forcing him to pray against his will does not help. It will only cause resentment, and you could lose him entirely. To be effective, an experience of salvation must be completely voluntary and without pressure. We must trust the Holy Spirit to do His work.

5. *Be specific.* Tell the pupil exactly what to do. If you want him to meet you after the class period is over, tell him exactly when and where. If he is ready to pray, help him. Have him repeat a simple prayer after you, expressing love and asking for forgiveness. Use short phrases and words he can understand.

Primaries, middlers, and juniors are sometimes referred to as being in the golden age for winning them to the Lord. Young people are eager to accept Christ, and you can touch their hearts (as well as the hearts of adults) if you will keep these five simple steps in mind. Utilizing them will result in a great spiritual harvest for the Lord. Once the new converts start bringing their friends, a continuous influx of new pupils will occur, resulting in continuous growth. God will richly bless your efforts when your priorities are right.

Double Your Attendance in 30 Days

One of the very best things that can heppen in a stagnant Sunday school is to structure a campaign that will draw on all the resources of the church. Get all the people working together to achieve what is believed to be an impossible goal, and then do it! What a thrill when everyone shares in the exhilaration of accomplishment. It will do wonders for your school!

1. *Set the date.* Target a Sunday for the highest attendance you have ever had. Some have used Easter, Mother's Day, Thanksgiving Sunday, and Christmas Sunday with great success. Once the Sunday is chosen, you must allow four weeks in order to reach your goal.

2. *Set your goal.* Determine what your average attendance has been for the past six months, then double it. Round off the goal to the next higher number. For example: 84 doubled would be 168. That should be rounded to become a goal of 175 or even 200.

3. *Order printing.* Design a card similar to the one shown at the end of the chapter (p.104). It is important that it has a stub to be removed. How many? You should order five times your goal.

4. *Post the goal.* Using construction paper, make large numbers to promote the goal. Place them on the walls of the foyer, classrooms, hallways, and rest rooms. If you have steps to another level, design a long, narrow sign for each riser, reading, "Step up to 200." The objective is to have everyone become conscious of the goal.

5. *Design a display.* Select a prominent wall, perhaps in the foyer where it is seen by most people, and prepare to display the names of everyone who promises to attend on Super Sunday. Have a large banner painted that says, "Super Sunday - April 22 - Be One of 200 In Attendance at First Assembly."

6. *Conduct a workers conference.* When the printed cards and displays are ready, have the Sunday school staff come together for an in-depth briefing. Explain procedures for using the cards, how the names will be posted on the display, and what awards will be given. Answer all questions so that everyone will clearly understand how the campaign works.

7. *Plan the awards.* Bibles, reference books, camp scholarships, dinner out, etc., are all quite acceptable awards. Plan an award for each class, from the junior level and up. It will go to the pupil who signs up the greatest number of visitors for Super Sunday.

8. *Begin promotion.* Six weeks before Super Sunday, start talking about it in every service. Publicize the launch date. Display the awards. Write the story in your weekly newsletter. Get excited about it!

9. *Launch the campaign.* Four Sundays before Super Sunday is launch date. Promote for a good attendance on that Sunday. A special guest would help attract members who do not attend regularly. At the close of Sunday school have every teacher take time to explain the program to the pupils. Give a card and pencil to each pupil, asking them to sign it. Each pupil present that day, from the primary classes up, will sign a card, detach the stub, and give it to the teacher.

For preschool classes you have two options: (1) Sign a card for the child and pin the reminder portion on their blouse or shirt, or (2) let each parent sign for the preschooler. Collect all stubs.

Next, give all pupils (juniors and up) a supply of cards and encourage them to get their friends to promise to come by signing a card. Give careful instructions for all stubs to be returned each Sunday. Display the awards to be given to the pupil who signs up the most.

10. *Post the names.* Every stub collected will be posted on the display in the foyer. By keeping a running count of the stubs displayed, you will know just how much work remains to be done to reach your goal. To insure victory on Super Sunday you will want to sign up at least 10 percent more than the number of your goal.

11. *Make the cards available.* Every Sunday when you collect the stubs, distribute more cards to each pupil. Be sure to sign up those present each Sunday who have not yet done so. Encourage everyone to recruit his friends.

12. *Target special groups.* Send young people after their peers in high school. If you have adults who attend worship but do not attend Sunday school, take time in the worship service to sign them up. Special visitor teams could move through the congregation after the service, signing new people up for the campaign. Give attention to the handicapped. Special arrangements should be made to transport them.

13. *Promote! Promote! Promote!* Talk it up! Everyone on the staff must be an enthusiastic supporter and follow through with procedures every Sunday.

14. *Organize a phone brigade.* This can become a special project for the young people. Divide the stubs into as many assignments as there are youth. Write a little message for them to read over the phone: "Hello! This is John Smith from First Assembly. Tomorrow is Super Sunday in our church, and we are all excited about the great crowd we are going to have. You are one of 200 who promised to come, and we are counting on you. See you at 9:30 tomorrow morning! Goodbye." Phone every person who signed a card, preferably on Saturday. This last minute reminder is very important!

15. *You are ready.* Having supported all your efforts by prayer, and by insuring that everyone is working together for the entire month to bring their friends, you are about to witness a remarkable victory. Classrooms will be crowded

with eager faces and hungry hearts. People will respond to the invitation and find a Saviour who loves and forgives. Everyone will rejoice together in the wonderful works of God. It will be great!

Big Sundays

In addition to two campaigns each year you will want to keep the momentum going by adding special "Big Sundays." Take a look at the calendar year. List the Sundays you think your attendance may be down. They might include the holiday Sundays (e.g., Memorial Day, Fourth of July, Labor Day). Identify vacation Sundays, family reunions, community events, and other activities that have a tendency to keep people away. Plan special promotions for these days.

Balloon Day. Everyone who comes gets a balloon to launch into the sky! Fill them with helium and attach a friendly message, with an offer of a reward when returned by the finder. It's exciting to watch them rise into the sky!

Kite Day. Everyone who comes gets a kite. This promotion is ideal for early March. Kids love kites! You can give them the kite one Sunday, and a ball of string the following Sunday. Consider having a kite flying contest.

Hospitality Sunday. Ask each family in your church to invite a family of their acquaintance to share Sunday school, church, and then Sunday dinner with them. Take time for each family to introduce their guests. Have special greeters at the door.

Homecoming Sunday. Send invitations to all the families who have come at some time to the church. Encourage members to bring unchurched relatives. Have Sunday dinner-on-the-ground. Don't forget the seniors and shut-ins in these efforts.

Car Packing Sunday. Remember when young people tried to see who could pack the most people into a Volkswagon? Offer an award to the one who brings the most in his car. Station wagons and vans should be ruled out, or be given a separate award. Don't limit the driver to one trip! Count everyone in the car, family and guests.

Picture Sunday. Some Sunday schools make this an annual event. Arrange with a photographer to take a group photo of the entire Sunday school. Offer a copy to all who bring three or more visitors that Sunday.

You can create a wide variety of interesting themes for Big Sundays, including, "Old-Fashioned Sunday," "Fall Roundup," "Stand Up For America Sunday," "Grandparents Sunday," and many, many more. Fit the emphasis to the need. Be creative. Try something different. Follow the basic pattern for planning, scheduling, decorating and promoting. Big Sundays can work wonders for your Sunday school.

SUPER SUNDAY
Yes! I'll be there
Sunday, April 22

Name _____
Address _____
City _____
Phone _____
Need transportation   yes ☐ no ☐

Detach now and return to church

SUPER SUNDAY
FIRST ASSEMBLY OF GOD
HOMETOWN, PA.

EASTER-APRIL 22

_____
SIGNATURE
Carry this in your wallet as a reminder.

9

The Value of Enrollment
and Recordkeeping

A good Sunday school moves smoothly and effortlessly, like a piece of well-oiled machinery. It seems that whatever is done proves successful, and all parts of the organization fit together perfectly. An observer might get the impression that only a few people are needed to supervise the functions and maintain harmony. Not so!

Behind the scenes are important people quietly doing their work, knowing exactly what their responsibilities are. Among this group of workers are the office secretaries. They are the guardians of the records, and are meticulous with the procedures and files so that every person is accounted for. Records mean people!

A good record system will open the front door to every person, and close the back door so none can get out. Any structured growth program must combine these two elements: (1) bringing new people in and (2) keeping them. Such a system requires more than a class record book.

Thousands of small Sunday schools' entire record system is the class record book, and it is stuffed into a drawer as soon as Sunday school is over. It is not thought of again until the next Sunday. For this Sunday school the only policy followed is tradition, and the only recordkeeping is marking a "P" or an "A" after each name. If you want your Sunday school to grow, you will have to do much more than that.

The purpose of this chapter is to explain a simple and understandable record system that will establish quality control of every name added to your rolls. It will be functional and systematic in reaching new people, bringing them in, and keeping them so that they can be trained as dedicated disciples of Christ.

The Office

Every church needs an office. It is the heart of all planning, procedures, and outreach. If you want to grow, an office merits a sizeable investment of time and money. More than just a table in the back corner or a closet under the stairway, the office should be an efficient room, as large as possible, well located and lighted. Here is a list of essential equipment:

Desk and chair
Worktable
Typewriter
Four-drawer file (letter or legal size)
4- by 6-inch card file (2- or 4-drawer)
Folding machine
Copier or duplicator
Mailing system

Setting Up the Files

1. *The Master Enrollment File.* This is usually a 4- by 6-inch card file, containing a card for each person. It is a data-gathering system designed to register the vital statistics of every person you enroll. You would begin well by using the Gospel Publishing House Enrollment Card #07-5312.

2. *The Mailing File.* This type of file will depend upon the equipment you decide to purchase. Smaller churches file names alphabetically; larger mailing lists are filed by zip code to facilitate bulk mailings. Many churches develop duplicate mailing files and keep one off the church premises in case of a fire.

3. *The Follow-Up File.* Proper visitation and follow-up cannot be done successfully without some kind of system to record what has been done. If your school uses the Crown loose-leaf records, you can easily file the follow-up reports each week in the letter file. A manila folder, one for each worker, is excellent. If visitation assignments are being used with the triplicate form, you will need a 4- by 6-inch drawer for the reports.

4. *The Prospect File.* There are numerous sources of good prospects for your Sunday school. You will develop a plan for collecting these names and filing them for assignment to visitation teams. Once again a 4- by 6-inch card works well.

A Simple Philosophy

If you are reading this book I assume you want your Sunday school to grow. The first rule of growth is very simple: new people have to come in. The second rule is equally simple: the people must keep coming. This seems oversimplified, but may be far more involved than it appears. Do you have convenient parking for the visitor? Will someone meet him at the door and give him directions to the proper class? Is the classroom clearly identified with the class name and the teacher's name on the door? If the visitor is required to discover everything on his own, it is very difficult and uncomfortable for him to come in.

After he is finally seated in the classroom you tell him he has to repeat this entire process for three consecutive Sundays before you will consider making him a member of your Sunday school. Why? Because you have always done it this way. It is the accepted tradition. You insist on his proving to you that he will be a faithful member before you will add his name to your class roll. You do not want any more absentees to follow up!

Now, let me share with you a very simple philosophy. When you adopt it, many of your procedures will be radically transformed. Here it is: *Make it easy to get in to your Sunday school and hard to get out*! Isn't that simple? Yet, scores of Sunday schools have this philosophy reversed. They make it hard to get in and easy to get out. This simple philosophy would tell us to add as many names as we can to our rolls, then develop procedures of follow-up that make it extremely difficult to remove a name from the rolls. We will discuss this more in the following paragraphs.

Three Laws Governing Numerical Growth

Several years ago our national Sunday School Department saw the need for strengthening the enrollment in every Sunday school as a basis for new growth. A plan was designed called Enrollment Plus. A complete manual is available from the national Sunday School Department.

Law One: The Law of Percentages

No way can you have 100 percent of your enrollment in attendance on any one Sunday. Some will be sick, some will be out of town, some will be in a situation when their commitment is weak and they may not come. Neither will you ever have 0 percent in attendance. No matter how dull the day or how bad the weather, the faithful will always show up.

Attendance fluctuates throughout the year. Big Sundays will produce high attendance, and bad weather will cause it to drop. However, when you average your attendance over the year you will discover that a given percentage will be in attendance each Sunday. The average is usually 70 percent. (Remember, we call this your Active Participation Rate: Your average attendance divided by your enrollment.)

Most superintendents and teachers try to *increase* the APR, that is, have fewer absentees. They believe this will make the records look better, reduce the work-load of follow-up, and the teachers will be happier. Surely our motives must be higher than just keeping teachers happy! If we spend time erasing names we are throwing people away! Develop a keen interest in people who do not regularly attend. Work on the chronic absentee. Building a reservoir of absentees *lowers* your APR and simultaneously provides you with the prospects you need for growth.

Law Two: The Law of Absentees

We have noted that you will always have some absentees. That number for the average Sunday school is approximately 30 percent of the enrollment. These absentees are just as important as the people who are present. When you begin to erase the absentees you are going to seriously affect your attendance. Here is a formula:

$$E \text{ (Enrollment}) = P \text{ (Present)} + A \text{ (Absent)}$$
$$100 = 70 + 30$$

When you want to permanently increase your attendance you must increase your enrollment. To double your attendance from 70 to 140 you must enroll 200 people. Then you are going to average 60 absentees every Sunday! You cannot have 140 present without having 60 absent. When you double your enrollment you double your attendance, and you also double your absentees.

People do not understand this law, so the first thing they want to do when they see a large number of absentees is clean the rolls. They erase the names of all who have not attended in the past six weeks or so. This is a terrible mistake! Often, when a new pastor comes into the church, or a new secretary assumes her responsibilities, the very first thing each of them does is update the rolls by erasing names, literally throwing people away. This brings us to our third law.

Law Three: The Law of Additions and Removals

We concentrate mostly on the absentees. It is the absentee who gets our attention. He is the one we talk about over Sunday dinner, wondering where he was. To mark a person absent more than four Sundays in a row is upsetting for a teacher. The teacher will often pressure the secretary, saying, "Do something. Take his name off the roll. It clutters up my book and it's a lot of bother to keep marking him absent." Why does the teacher want the name erased? Because each time she marks him absent, she feels some guilt for having done little or nothing to get him back in class!

You could do exactly what this teacher wants and remove the names of all who are absent. Then everyone would be relieved. You could more easily achieve 100 percent attendance with no absentees. Great! But for how long? Remember Law One and your APR. This procedure of erasing names and purging the rolls is killing Sunday schools all over America.

Don't ever forget that when your enrollment increases, your attendance will increase. When your enrollment decreases, your attendance will decrease. Guard your enrollment carefully! When was the last time you had it carefully checked? You should follow your enrollment as closely as you follow your attendance.

Now we come to a most important question: When should we add names, and when should we remove names? *Adding Names.* Remember our simple philosophy—easy to get in and hard to get out. You should make it a matter of policy to add as many names as possible just as fast as you can. Scratch the old idea of coming three consecutive Sundays before becoming a member. Get a map of your county and, using your town as the center, inscribe a circle on the map with a 10-mile radius. (More if you like.) Every unchurched person living within this circle becomes a potential member of your Sunday school. This becomes your constituent area. Do everything you can to make contact with every potential member. The very first time people come to visit your Sunday school make them a member. In fact, it would be better to identify them as new members, rather than visitors. The true visitors in your Sunday school are those who come from outside your constituent area. They are relatives or friends who attend some other church, and they have come for only one time.

The procedure is simple. Prepare a *new member* card. Ask for the same information requested on the enrollment card that is kept in the master file. Blank cards are available to all teachers at all times. If you have a receptionist at a welcome desk, she should have a supply of them. If you are involved in the bus ministry, the triplicate form used to keep attendance on the bus is quite suitable for collecting this information. However the new member may come, you must secure this vital information either on the bus, at the welcome desk, or in the classroom. You must not allow a single new person to come into your Sunday school without obtaining this information. Make this a matter of policy. These new member cards are to be sent to the office for processing on Monday.

The office secretary will do five important things with these cards:

1. Add the new name to the master file. Using the master enrollment card, she will transfer all this information to that card and add it to the active file, usually alphabetically.

2. Add the new name to the class roll. She will add the new name to the appropriate class roll by means of the class book or the loose-leaf sheet.

3. Add the new name to the mailing list. You may want to group these names into families, or leave them single.

4. Send a letter of welcome. This can be a form letter, but it should not be mimeographed. It should be carefully and warmly worded, acknowledging the new member's attendance, and urging him to return next Sunday. The pastor should sign it. This letter must be sent no later than Monday morning.

5. Assign someone to visit the home. Sometimes this can be the teacher, but more often it is a selected and trained visitation team. This visit must be made during the week following the first Sunday of attendance. The new person is a

new member and the best prospect you can ever hope to have for Sunday school growth. Don't fail in this follow-up.

For those living outside your constituent area (the true visitors) you will proceed with numbers 3 and 4, adding their names to your mailing list, and sending them a letter of welcome.

Removing Names. Again, remember our simple philosophy —make it easy to get in and hard to get out. You should have a policy that says you will do all within your power to reach and win the people on your rolls. Set no time limit. Permit a name to remain on the roll as long as it is necessary. Urge teachers, visitation teams, and any others engaged in follow-up to do their best. Commit this effort to prayer. Trust the guidance of the Holy Spirit. Be persistent. In the long run you will see the benefits of this effort.

Some names can be removed quickly, such as those who die, those who move away, and those who tell you they are regularly attending another church. You need not hesitate to remove these names.

All other names should be removed only after you have done your best in follow-up, and that can be determined only by you. At some point you must ask yourself whether you can continue using your time trying to reach someone who continues to reject you. Would it not be better to direct your efforts to others who may be receptive? Only you can decide this, and the decision will be different for each person.

When the time comes to remove a name, it should be done only in the office. Teachers should never erase names. The secretary will take the name off the class roll and remove the enrollment card from the master file. Do not throw the card away. Instead, place it in an inactive master file. Keep the name on the mailing list and continue to send regular mailings to them. During times of special outreach campaigns this inactive master file will yield many good prospects for another try. You will discover that over a period of time, some new member cards coming into the office will already have a card in your inactive master file. You need only place it back in the active master file and begin all over again these five important steps for all new members.

FOLLOW-UP

Any type of program initiated by your Sunday school for growth *must* include follow-up or its effectiveness will be limited. Every good salesman knows the importance of follow-up. If he ignored the "callbacks" and discarded his prospect file he would soon be out of business. Many good Sunday schools realize this. They have earnestly tried, but have found traditional programs of follow-up to be unproductive. Let's be pragmatic as we look at this very important element for growth.

Focus On the Absentee

The absentees' names on your Sunday school enrollment present one of your greatest challenges. However, most Sunday school workers view absentees as troublesome at best. There are the occasional absentees, absent only because of illness or vacation. These are often simply overlooked. Then, there are the habitual absentees. These are the ones who show up for class once or twice a month. When this person is absent the teacher feels pangs of conscience. *Did I do something to offend him?* she asks herself. She knows she should contact him, but that is disruptive to her own schedule, and she finds it difficult to take the time. The teacher reasons, *Wouldn't it be nice if every pupil were present every Sunday?* Then we would know exactly how to prepare for each session and everything would run more smoothly. Altogether, the absentees are something we could do without.

But wait! We must see the absentee through the eyes of Jesus. Remember the story of the shepherd who had a hundred sheep? When he brought them into the fold at evening one was missing. Did he get angry? Did that sheep create problems for the shepherd? It surely did. He had to leave the ninety-nine safe in the fold while he went out into the night in search of the one that was lost. But he found the lost sheep and his work as the shepherd was fulfilled. Disruptive? Yes! It was the shepherd heart that compelled him to go after the one that was lost. When the Sunday school worker has a shepherd heart, he will go after the absentee with a loving, searching persistence until the absent one is found.

A growing Sunday school is like a series of concentric circles. Every church has a solid group of committed, responsible people. They make up the working staff for the Sunday school, and you can always count on them to attend. This group is the center circle. Around this responsible group is a second circle representing those who are absent one or two Sundays a month. They show interest in spiritual matters and participate in most class activities, but they are people who lack commitment.

A third group forms another even larger circle. This group attends only when something special is scheduled. They want to retain their identity with your church but they come only when it is convenient.

Using the plan for adding names to the roll as fast as possible you can add another circle. The fourth circle represents the people who have come once, and have made your church responsible for them by adding their names to the roll. It is from these expanding fringe groups that you draw people to win to Christ. This is where your work really is. You must see these people as important to your growth and not just as absentees. They are your best prospects for the kingdom of God and membership in your church. A good follow-up program will give diligent attention to the fringes.

Find the Prospects

Search your Sunday school rolls. If you have been in the habit of throwing away names and terminating members arbitrarily, an examination of old records will yield a gold mine of prospects. The Enrollment Plus program tells of one pastor who found such a list of ninety names. When he evaluated them, 30 should have been removed because they had died, moved, or changed their church membership. The remaining 60 were contacted and within three weeks half of them were back in Sunday school.

Use "people webs." Everyone attending your Sunday school knows someone who does not attend anywhere. These are friends, neighbors, relatives and other acquaintances. The newer the convert, the greater the number of his unchurched friends. Prepare some prospect cards and periodically distribute them to all members of your youth and adult classes. Do this at the beginning of a Sunday session with instructions to write the name and address of someone who is unchurched. New converts will want several cards. Do this on a regular basis and you will develop a prospect file rapidly.

People are always moving into your town. Devise a way to secure the names of these people and add their names to your prospect file. Establish a contact with the realtors, the utilities, and other public services. Your own members can be constantly alert to newcomers in the community.

Follow Up the Absentees and Prospects

Pray. There is power in prayer. Reaching these chronic absentees and unlocking the hearts of prospects requires constant, fervent prayer. "Praying always with all prayer and supplication in the Spirit. . ." is the injunction of Paul to the Ephesians (Ephesians 6:18). It is like the artillery bombardment that softens up the enemy lines before the foot soldiers move in. Through prayer God touches the heart and prepares the way for those who engage in follow-up. Make lists of your absentees and prospects to be distributed among the people who gather for prayer. Have them pray for these people by name. Earnest prayer like this will soften their resistance and make your follow-up more productive.

Phone. Almost everyone has a telephone, and it can be used very conveniently and effectively for follow-up. Teachers can occasionally phone an absentee to express concern and love. Teens can phone their friends and invite them to Sunday school. During growth campaigns a "telephone blitz" can be used effectively. Regular members can be phoned periodically to prevent absenteeism. Phone conversations should always be very positive, to the point, and brief.

Write. Personal letters and notes are always welcome. Teachers can use personalized notes, cards, and letters to affirm their concern and love. They need not be lengthy. Children especially enjoy getting letters, as well as youth and adults. Reminder letters can go out from the superintendent to absentees announcing some special occasion. The pastor can send personal letters to the prospects, inviting them to attend. Mimeographed letters should be used only for very large mailings, and then they should be professionally done.

A common phenomenon in our churches today is the large number of adults who come for the morning worship service, but have little interest in Sunday school. The names of these adults should be secured and a special mailing program planned for them. Choose an elective subject you think would be attractive to them, for example, "The Christian Home," "The Christian and His Money." Design a one-sheet summary of the lessons with some Bible references and questions. Make them appealing. Write a letter to each of these adults announcing the series of special lessons designed for them. Two letters should be sent prior to the beginning of the series, with the second letter containing the first lesson sheet. If the prospect fails to attend the first lesson, send him another invitation with the second lesson summary. Be persistent. All letters should be sent first class.

Visit. Remember the Gallup survey about unchurched Americans quoted in chapter 7? There are vast numbers of unchurched adults in every community who will come if you will only invite them. Many of these adults can be identified through "people webs" and placed in your prospect file. The people who submit the names of adults as prospects should be encouraged to make the first visit to invite them to Sunday school. Subsequent visits can be made by special visitation teams through assignments. These visitation teams are recruited and trained especially for this type of outreach.

Teachers should be encouraged to visit habitual absentees when it is possible. Certain seasons of the year lend themselves to this emphasis, and motivation for the task can be provided in a workers conference. Visiting the absentee encourages him and strengthens the teacher. Frequently, others in the family who are unchurched can be brought into the Sunday school through such a personal visit.

A continuous visitation program of any type is very difficult to sustain. People grow weary of the task and find themselves too busy. Knowing this, the pastor and superintendent will call the workers to a renewed commitment periodically, and the entire staff can renew their efforts to reach out to people. Committed workers will always see people as Jesus saw them, "scattered abroad, as sheep having no shepherd" (Matthew 9:36). With His help you can find these people and bring them into the fold.

10

Maintaining Growth

America is a land of churches! Beautiful new churches, adequate for reaching people, proclaim the good news in faith and power. Stately old cathedrals with weather-marked walls stand as mute testimony of long years of witness to a world needing Christ. Countless "average" neighborhood churches dot the landscape in every town and village where you will find the faithful gathered every Sunday. New "first unit" churches of new congregations affirm the excitement of the Christian faith in an effort to share the gospel with their world. Our country has no shortage of churches!

A closer look at these churches reveals a wide difference in their vitality. Some are lively, growing Sunday schools, vibrant in their continuing efforts to reach people. Their facilities utilize activities designed for evangelism and healing the hurts of people. On the other hand, you will discover many Sunday schools with a static enrollment, having reached a certain plateau and unable to move beyond it. Still others are plagued with apathy and indifference, faced with declining enrollments, and struggling for their very existence! Can a Sunday school reverse its direction, throw off its dying image, and emerge among the ranks of vibrant, growing churches? Yes! The following discussion will tell how it can happen.

Evaluate Your Current Status

A good Sunday school will carefully consider every area of its total program. As an example of how to examine one particular area, we will discuss attendance. Be totally honest. Trace your attendance on a graph for the past five years. Ask where you are going? Can you see any trends?

High points on the graph are likely indicating some growth caused by a particular effort or promotion. But your attendance may have drifted back to its original level. A good Sunday school campaign, planned and executed by a team of enthusiastic workers, will increase the attendance in almost any Sunday school. Too often, however, it is a rise that soon dissipates. These Sunday schools are like a giant sieve — people are merely passing through.

Real growth is measured by progress toward a goal. The Sunday school goal is reaching people, winning them to Christ, discipling them, and incorporating them into the church as members. This is very specific, and the first step involves building attendance. Sporadic growth is unacceptable, for it will generally be lost. We must develop procedures that will hold the increase.

Everyone knows of a church that had 50 in attendance last Sunday, 50 last week, 50 last month, 50 last year, 50 five years ago! No matter what they do they always seem to have 50. They are on a plateau and have never discovered what needs to be done to move higher. Too many Sunday schools have established themselves in this position and have been there for years. If you can identify the plateau your Sunday school is on, then apply the measures necessary to move ahead. You *can* experience growth.

A check of the Assemblies of God Annual Church Ministries Reports will reveal distinct plateaus around which churches tend to cluster. They can be identified at 50, 70, 90, 120, 180, and 230. Large numbers of churches seem to be stuck at these levels, especially the lower ones.

In his book, *The Pyramid Principle of Church Growth**
David Womack identifies plateaus similar to these and explains why they occur. Almost any church can get fifty

*This book is no longer in print.

people together. Ten to twelve families will make up such a congregation, and often, some of the families are related. They probably worship in a small, aging building that is comfortable for their size. They have four or five Sunday school classes. Finances are limited. Often the building is in disrepair. The pastor is usually employed outside the church as income is insufficient to pay him a salary. He does everything, from preaching to performing the custodial duties. After a while he gets discouraged and leaves. Few unchurched people in the community are willing to identify with such a small, closely related group. However, if this pastor and his people can work together with enthusiasm and excitement to reach new people they have an excellent chance for seeing the attendance increase. They must turn their focus away from themselves and internal problems, and concentrate on reaching new people. When they do, the next plateau is not far off!

When the church enrollment reaches 70, there is again the danger that growth will stabilize. Even though the building has been painted and the sign out front has been modernized, even though a Sunday school superintendent has begun working closely with the pastor and two new classes have been started—the pastor is still doing all the work around the church. Usually families have emerged in key positions in the church. Their positions are threatened by every new person who now comes into the church, especially if the newcomer has ability. Hence, the congregation has the tendency to treat the newcomer coolly; he does not feel welcome.

These people must be revived with a new vision and understanding of the Great Commission. When they realize the first task of the church is winning souls they will lay aside the me-first attitude and direct their efforts to others. Changing direction on this plateau is one of the greatest challenges a pastor can face. It will demand help only the Holy Spirit can give.

The next plateau is well known as typical for many

Assemblies of God churches. At 90 in Sunday school attendance, the church building remains closed except at service times. The pastor is still doing most of the work, except that now his wife is probably the unpaid secretary. On the bulletin board is a rotating list of people each month who staff the nursery, the children's church, and take care of custodial duties. The choir sings only at Easter and Christmas.

This church has reached the limits of what one man can do, and unless it begins to recruit and train workers for specific tasks, it will remain at this level. If that happens, certain cliques will develop to work against any meaningful growth. The pastor must be a leader in establishing training programs for the laity that will equip them to accept key roles in the body, including outreach.

If that happens, the church will grow to the next plateau. When the church has reached 120, the pastor usually has moved his office into the church and now has regular hours there. Usually regular morning hours are kept at the building each day. The church music program is improving and the choir sings more frequently. Several new Sunday school classes have been added, and the facilities are filled. The pastor directs regular workers conferences to keep the lines of communication and training open. The pastor's wife is still the secretary, though there is talk of hiring someone full-time. Most other work around the church is performed by volunteers.

When the Sunday school reaches this plateau, great excitement is present and, occasionally, someone will suggest that more space is needed. This is the direction the entire leadership of the church should be looking. When additional space is acquired, more Sunday school classes can be added to provide opportunities for the laity to be trained. The pastor and other leaders should become very aggressive about acquisition of space. Otherwise, the momentum that has been established will be lost. The people will settle into a comfortable routine designed to hold what gains you have, and outreach will suffer.

Once additional space is acquired, it usually fills quickly, propelling attendance to the next plateau of 180. The church will now have a full-time secretary and custodian. The church office will be active all week, busy with procedures required to increase and sustain the growth. Mailings need to be prepared, files kept, bulletins and newsletters printed, records processed, and assignments made for follow-up. The Sunday school is supervised by an efficient and enthusiastic superintendent who works closely with a dedicated Christian education committee. Things run smoothly. New faces appear every Sunday in the classes. Excitement is contagious. The choir sings every Sunday morning. The calendar is full of social activities and events for every age. Most important, people are finding Christ each week.

It is my feeling that churches moving through these plateaus make a frequent mistake by hiring associate ministers of music, youth, and Christian education long before they are really needed. They reason that hiring associates will strengthen those particular areas of ministry and thereby produce growth. This is not necessarily true. Most pastors have the ability to lead a growing congregation up to 250 without hiring full-time associates. The real key to getting the work done is to assign as much detailed work as possible to trained laity, a full-time secretary, and a custodian. Many pastors of large, fast-growing churches suggest the hiring of a second secretary before bringing in associate ministers.

Expand the Base

David Womack uses the pyramid as the working model of a growing church. He observes that the only way you can build a pyramid larger is to first expand the base. Suppose you have a pyramid of sand on a table top. There is no way you can pile the sand higher without making the base larger. As you pour the sand on the pyramid, the base expands as the mass increases. The base will continue to expand as long as the table is large enough to hold it. Then growth will stop. This is a good illustration of a growing church, and the sequence is the same. First, expand the base: the organization and administration. Then you will increase the mass: the attendance. When the table—the building—cannot hold any more, growth stops.

Review the previous paragraphs in this chapter and assess the current position of your Sunday school. In these paragraphs you will find subtle suggestions of what you must do to expand your base. Without being too simplistic, identify one or two areas where you need correction, then start. Don't wait until every area is analyzed and detailed plans developed—that could take a long time and leave you frustrated. Start with what is most obvious. Go as far as you can see, and when you get there, you can see farther.

Don't be a perfectionist. Don't wait for conditions to be perfect before you start, for they never will be. You may not have all the know-how, sufficient workers, or enough money, but go ahead and do what you can with what you have. Lots of mistakes will be made along the way, but don't fear them. When you make an error, it is evident you have tried to do something. The only person who doesn't make mistakes is the one who never does anything! Nothing is ever going to "just happen." You have to make it happen! Nothing will ever be attempted for God if all possible objections must first be overcome.

Develop a Positive Atmosphere

The general attitude of the people develops an atmosphere in the church that becomes very obvious to the visitor. Discouragement, problems, criticism, and other negative responses are detrimental to growth. Have faith! Believe that God can and will help you to achieve success. Build positive morale. This is done as the leadership develops a positive, caring attitude and helps the church staff do the same. Keeping things on a high level of morale is important to growth.

Every church has a personality, and the personality of your church is the sum-total of the attitudes of the people who attend. When people have a godly attitude, they will be warm and friendly, developing the atmosphere necessary for growth. Fruit grows and ripens when the atmosphere is right. A cold wave will kill everything!

Get the Laity Involved

A critical component of creating a growth pattern in your church is a high level of lay involvement. Great churches are never built by one person. Strong leadership is essential, but so is active lay involvement. Begin with the people you have, regardless of the number. Set up training sessions in which you share visions and goals with them. Don't be frustrated by those who refuse to participate. Work with those who are willing. Then, reach out for new people.

Plan job opportunities that are meaningful and provide responsibility. Elevate qualifications and responsibilities to make every job a genuine challenge. People will rise to a challenge! You need workers to build attendance; the more workers you have, the more people will be reached and won to the Lord. As a rule of thumb, for every worker on your staff you can expect between seven and ten people present in Sunday school each week.

Set Goals

The leadership must believe that God wants the Sunday school to grow and that belief must be built in the hearts of the people. Setting goals for the work of the Lord is a very spiritual activity in which you must be involved.

When Moses assumed leadership of Israel, his goal was to lead his people out of bondage into the land of promise. He fell short of his goal because of unbelief. When Joshua took command of the troops, his goal was the conquest of Canaan. Some of the tribes wanted to stop short of that goal and take up residence east of Jordan, but they were allowed to only after they agreed to fight until the ultimate goal was achieved.

The Great Commission is a goal set by our Lord himself for every believer. Acts 1:8 is a clear goal for the church, "Ye shall be witnesses . . . both in Jerusalem, and in all Judea, and in Samaria, and unto the uttermost part of the earth." The Cross was God's goal in sending His Son into the world. Even now, God's goal for the whole world is the return of His Son to become King of kings and Lord of lords!

Goal setting is an important part of spiritual leadership. When you look for the key that causes Sunday schools to launch out on a course of growth, you will find it to be goal setting. Sunday schools that don't have goals are failing and those that set goals are succeeding.

A drifting ship gets nowhere. You can load a ship with cargo, start its engines, and pull in the anchor—but with no captain and crew on board who know where they are going, the ship will scarcely get out of the harbor. And if by chance it should drift out of the harbor to the open seas, it will surely be dashed to pieces on the rocks. You must make a choice. Will you just let your Sunday school drift? Or will you set some meaningful goals that will chart a course for you?

Here are four things to keep in mind as you set goals for your Sunday school:

1. Goals must be ambitious. God is a big God! Daniel said, "But the people that do know their God shall be strong, and do exploits" (Daniel 11:32). This verse is found in the middle of a chapter describing terrible tribulations. If you think things are tough now, start thinking big! Create some excitement! In sports, a team always performs better against tough competition than against a mediocre team.

2. Goals must be daily. If you do not have daily objectives you qualify as a dreamer. If you really expect to accomplish growth you must work toward that goal every day. A mother brings a new baby into the world as a helpless

infant. She knows that child will someday become a responsible adult, but years of labor come first. It becomes a series of daily chores to care for the child, teaching him carefully, until he finally emerges as an adult. Your goal can only be achieved as you work at it every day.

3. You should also have long range goals. There will be plenty of short range frustrations to pull you off course, unless you have long-range goals that are like a compass to maintain positive direction in spite of the storm.

4. Goals must be specific. Take the hottest day, a magnifying glass, and a pile of papers. You will never ignite the papers with the glass if you keep the glass moving. When you focus and hold it on one spot, a blaze will appear in a matter of seconds. Spell out exactly what you want to accomplish. Avoid generalities. A "big" Sunday school, "more" teachers, a "better" building, reaching a "lot" of people—none of these will lead to achievement. Whether it be attendance building or evangelism, establish goals for it with actual numbers and specific dates attached.

Call a meeting of your Christian education committee for the purpose of goal setting. Give each person a piece of paper and ask him to make a list of things he would like to see the Sunday school accomplish in the next 6 months. To help you get started, here are some questions to ask:

How many people would you like to see converted?
What facilities would you like to improve?
What equipment do you want to purchase?
Do you need more space? How much? For what?
How many new classes would you like to start?
How many new workers would you like to enlist?
How many new bus routes would you like to establish?
What attendance record would you like to set? When?
Which area would you like to reorganize? When?
What visitation program would you like to begin? When?

Make your list as long as you can. When it is complete, have each member of the committee place an "X" by the six items he thinks are most important. Do not take any time to study or discuss this. It must be done quickly.

When the lists have been checked, write all of them on a chalkboard. You will discover both differences and similarities. Discuss the list on the chalkboard in detail and decide, as a committee, which six matters will be undertaken first. Transfer these to cards for each member of the committee. Ask each person to make a commitment to pray daily and specifically for the six items. Seek God for His leadership and direction as you plan definite steps to achieve your objectives.

By doing this, you will do what very few Sunday schools ever do. You have set meaningful, specific goals. Next, implement the goals you have set.

Call the committee together in 2 to 4 weeks, after each member has carefully prayed for God's direction. When you meet, be prepared to listen attentively to every suggestion made as to what course of action should be taken.

Don't underestimate any idea you hear. Think optimistically. Once the committee is dedicated to reaching their goals by whatever route God will direct, the planning and the work is actually fun!

Just the mention of the word *change* makes some people nervous. It creates resistance. Few people like change, yet growth demands it. Like people, Sunday schools acquire bad habits, and changing an old habit is usually difficult. People may get upset or even hostile, so make all changes gradually. It is like a sick person taking medicine. He takes a spoonful at a time rather than the whole bottle.

Luke deliberately left the Acts of the Apostles unfinished. The last chapter ends abruptly, as if he, or some future writer, would again pick up the pen and continue that glorious history of the church. None of us can realize what contributions we are making to that history, but when the final chapter is written, I trust it will include the story of how you increased the kingdom of God through your efforts in Sunday school.

Bibliography

Arn, Winfield C., and Arn, Charles. *Master's Plan for Making Disciples*. Pasadena, CA: Church Growth Press, 1982.

Bisagno, John R. *How to Build an Evangelistic Church*. Nashville: Broadman Press, 1971.

Engstrom, Ted W. *Making of a Christian Leader*. Grand Rapids, MI: Zondervan Publishing House, 1976.

Graf, Arthur. *The Church in the Community*. Grand Rapids, MI: Wm. B. Eerdmans Publishing Company, 1965.

Hamilton, Michael. *God's Plan for the Church-Growth*. Springfield, MO: Gospel Publishing House, 1981.

Hoge, Dean R. and Roozen, David A. *Understanding Church Growth and Decline*. New York, Philadelphia, 1979.

Jones, Ezra E. *Strategies for New Churches*. New York: Harper & Row Publishers, 1976.

Kelly, Dean M. *Why Conservative Churches Are Growing*. New York: Harper & Row Publishers, 1972.

McGavran, Donald, and Arn, Winfield, C. *How to Grow a Church*. Glendale, CA: Regal Books, 1973.

McGavran, Donald, and Arn, Winfield C. *Ten Steps for Church Growth*. New York: Harper & Row Publishers, 1977.

McGavran, Donald; Arn, Charles; Arn, Win. *Growth, A New Vision for the Sunday School*. Pasadena, CA: Church Growth Press, 1980.

McGavran, Donald, and Hunter, George. *Church Growth: Strategies That Work*. Nashville: Abingdon Press, 1980.

Rusbuldt, Richard; Gladden, Richard, and Green, Norman Jr. *Local Church Planning Manual*. Valley Gorge, PA: Judson Press, 1978.

Towns, Elmer. *The Complete Book of Church Growth*. Wheaton, IL: Tyndale House, 1982.

Wagner, Peter. *Our Kind of People: The Ethical Dimensions of Church Growth in America*. Atlanta: John Knox Press, 1979.

Wagner, Peter. *What Are We Missing?* Carol Streams, IL: Creation House, Inc., 1973.

Wagner, Peter. *Your Church Can Grow*. Glendale, CA: Regal Books, 1976.

Westing, Harold J. *Make Your Sunday School Grow Through Evaluation*. Wheaton, IL: Victor Books, 1977.

Womack, David. *Breaking the Stained Glass Barrier*. New York: Harper & Row Publishers, 1973.